1

5F: Portraits

Learn about realism.

Graeme Smith

PUBLISHED ON AMAZON.com
by
LABYRINTH BOOKS

DEDICATION:

This book is dedicated to my family.
Hele-ly (Ly).
        my wife:

Ingrid.
        our daughter:

Marie.
        my former wife:

Fiona, Natalie and Michael
        our children:

Georgie
        Michael's wife:

Pearl, Kiki and Martha.
        their children:

They have put up with me for many years and I thank them for that.
I hope this book gives an insight into what occupied me much of the time.
All have done worthwhile and interesting things in the absence of my help.
I congratulate them for their achievements.

SUPPORT:

Support the International Artist magazine
– contact: editor@internationalartist.com

Support the Australian Artist magazine
– contact: editor@australianartist.com

HOW TO USE THIS BOOK.

Usually people don't think through things to the level they need to.
Because of that, they have projects instead of tasks on their "to do" list.
That leads to procrastination because it hasn't been broken down to a task level.
So go through your book once to understand it then go through it again.

Start at the PART of the book that you think you should start at.
Make notes of the steps you will need to take and the resources required.
Use the notes to make a step by step system to implement the particular ideas.
You don't have to refer back to the original, if you've created YOUR system.

The first question you have to ask and answer is "Why is this being done?"
How does this align with where you want to get to?
What are the strategic implications of doing this?
Does this fit in with getting to your goal in the shortest and fastest amount of time?
What would it be like if it were totally successful?
Define it - what is success for this project and how will you know?

Now brainstorm all the tasks are involved.
It's important not to go linear too fast, step 1, step 2, step 3, and step 4.
You end up cutting off options.
As you plan step 1, 2, and 3, there is a specific step that might be number 4.
If you start steps too quickly, other ways of doing 1, 2 and 3 may not appear.

The first 1/3 of a brainstorming session is easy - just generate lots of ideas.
The second third is a little bit more challenging.
Go through those ideas and see where they lead to.
Then push yourself to think outside the box for that's often where the big idea is!
That's where the most powerful way of getting the project done the fastest – is.

Most never get to that level and so end up short-changing themselves.
Then their project takes longer and they also set themselves up to procrastinate.
This final brainstorming part of the equation is incredibly important.

Once you fully brainstorm a project put your options into a linear sequence.
Then you can figure out what you've overlooked and everything becomes obvious.
Get your tasks in order, add missing steps, lay out your task list for the project.

Organize tasks in a linear way and decide what things to start immediately?
Step one is to start with no dependency on things that have to occur before them.
There might be step 5 or 6 or 20 that don't rely on anything else to get done.
You can get started on them right away!

Write what you think of at the time and also cross off things as you do them.
Add in stuff that is relevant from time to time.

As a basis for learning about realism use photographs.

Focus on learning what you can.
Action with materials = technique.
Practiced techniques = skill.
Habitual technique + skill = style.

Continue with the subject matter you want to paint really well.
That way you are continuing down the correct path (for you).
Your focus is always on portraits, landscapes, the sea, or whatever you like.

Don't just select animals focus on one (tiger, cat, horse).
Then even from the start you can become a specialist.
Also focus on something you are interested in.
This will help maintain the necessary motivation while you learn.

Understand your animal, house, landscape, or whatever you choose.
Over time you will develop the individual paining skills needed.
You will also know how to paint your subject your way.

Eventually you can focus on another subject.
If it is related to your original theme you will learn much quicker.
From one breed of dog to another is an example.
Then from one kind of animal to another.

You'll note the similarities and also the differences.
You could even progress from portraits to head and shoulders studies.
Later these might be full figures.
Follow this pattern for long enough, and you'll be able to paint anything!

People who do things well also do them faster than those who don't.
That applies to painting just as much as anything else.
It's one of the indicators of skill.

By now you should notice that repetition helps skill development.
Several small paintings are better for learning.
Larger ones take more time and that's how you apply what you have learnt.

Skill in art, sport or even medicine is basically the same phenomenon.

It's practiced behaviour in action.

Most artists don't do anywhere near enough to develop any real skill.

INDEX: PORTRAITS.

PORTRAITS

1. PORTRAITS

2. OBSERVED PORTRAITS

3. IMAGINARY PORTRAITS

An artist who lived in California wanted to learn how to paint polar bears.
In addition his painting skills were quite modest.
I suggested he do many small experimental studies by looking at photographs.
It didn't matter if they're finished or not for they were ways to learn about bears.

After 250 studies his first painting without a polar bear or a photograph.
He was totally surprised at how well his polar bear turned out.
Also the standard of the work was infinitely better than it had been in the past.
He had internalized his learning.
The polar bears he created were not a photographer's either as they were his!

As a way to learn about realism use photographs (at least to start with).
Any photograph is of something.
Instead of selecting random subject matter select the kind you'd like to paint.

If you want to learn to paint portraits, then choose facial photographs.
So like the Californian artist don't just select any focus on one.
Then even from the start you can become a specialist.

You get to understand portraits.
Over time you will develop the individual paining skills needed.
You will also know how to paint your subject your way.

Eventually you can focus on another subject.
If it is related to your original theme you will learn much quicker.
Focus on one sex then later the other is an example of portrait focus.

You'll note the similarities and also the differences.
You could go from portraits to head and shoulders studies and then full figures.
Follow this pattern for long enough, and you'll be able to paint anyone!

People who do anything well also do it faster than those who don't.
That applies to painting as much as anything else, it's an indicator of skill.

Skill in art, sport or even medicine is basically the same phenomenon.
It's practiced behaviour in action.
Most artists don't do anywhere near enough paintings to develop any real skill.
Many small experiments will beat one or two major efforts every time.

But you must do the 'hard yards'!
Painting a large number of experiments develops painting skill, and attitude.
You'll become more discerning, because you acquire more experience.
You'll not need, nor want, other people's assessments.

A number of experiments at the same time increases productivity.
For you reduce wasted time.
If you run into a dead-end with one painting move to another for a fresh start.
When the initial painting is returned to, there will be a different attitude.
Otherwise set it aside again.

Working on a number of paintings at the same time also saves materials.
A particular colour can be applied to the work for which it was intended.
BUT there are bound to be other works where that same colour is appropriate.

When you buy paint, buy in quantity, but only use as needed.

Can't remember what you did before then do whatever you think of now.
In the end it doesn't matter!
Usually you'll find most works will finish fresh and roughly about the same time.

Avoid major works.
They take time (years), usually done slowly and are often large and complex.
You'll tend to labour over them as you seek to do your best.
You learn to paint by painting.
You do not learn by someone telling you what to do.
That way you learn they know what to do and if you get stuck you ask them.

But you can also learn by looking.
That's how you learn about the appearance of things.
Traditional art learning is based on looking and putting.

It's possible to learn many simple things and gradually combine them.
A problem is that you can only paint what you can see.
But by actually painting such things you get to understand their appearance.
You also develop skill at depicting those you do most.

Let your experiments evolve.
Those that don't work out won't matter as you learn a great deal from 'failures'.
You'll learn what to do and what not to do next time.

Regard these as exercises or studies or experiments.
They are never going to be framed, sold or kept for posterity.
Just do many and do them reasonably quickly.

The Magic Multiple Miniatures is where you can't make a mistake.
Find out how they turn out - a discovery rather than reproducing something.

This is particularly useful when you are observing fleeting moments.
Sometimes they'll turn out great, but at other times not so.
But you don't need to be brave for there is no risk.

Do enough fleeting experiments and they WILL get better!
You will be able to capture in paint moments of life.
They have spontaneity that's often lacking in a photographic based artwork.

If you want to learn to paint portraits - then paint portraits.
BUT do NOT worry about how they turn out.
Just paint them and in time they'll improve but maybe you don't believe this?
I know a lady who is a fashion illustrator.
When she was a girl she used to draw people who were on TV.
She became both very good and also quick.

Once I tested an art education program in an elementary school.
The teaching process was closely linked to the materials issued to the pupils.
The particular material combinations chosen were not random.
They were designed to introduce some quite specific experiences to the pupils.
Their challenge was to see what they could create with any given combination.

One teacher noticed a particular boy over a series of lessons.
In the earliest lessons there were always two blobs present in the work.
It didn't matter what he was given by the teacher.
Over a period of time these blobs gradually changed into two birds.
They were just basic symbol-type birds, such as most people might do.

As the lessons continued the birds improved.
There were more details and eventually were recognizable as budgerigars.
No matter what materials he was given the boy did budgerigars.
The teacher tried to find materials that couldn't become budgerigars.

The boy always found a way to make the birds.
One time he even pin-pricked budgerigars onto paper.
What chance this kid might become the best budgerigar artist in the world?
If he continued, I'd say every chance.

Why did he do this?
Well the teacher discovered (surprise) he had two pet budgerigars.
They meant more to this boy than anything else.
The teacher DIDN'T tell him what to do so he could use his own knowledge.
He also got much better at it!

That's how it should be learning to paint portraits if that's what you want.
Just do them for they'll improve provided the motivation is strong enough.
It's also how you can develop confidence!
Imagine and learn new ways.
An artist, during the act of creating a work is expressing something.
Expression is a unique personal action.

Three artists attempt to paint the same subject, exactly as seen.
They will finish with three different works.
The differences can be attributed to the various artists' expression.
Their works are symbols for this expression.

Expression is related to emotion.
Although the individual may not be conscious of what that emotion is.
The presence of emotion creates a tension (a feeling).
The tension isn't that emotion, but an awareness of an emotional state.

Expression is bringing into perceptual form symbols for that awareness.
It is thus related to that the underlying emotional state.

The expressive act is not necessarily related to any particular audience.
There's a difference if intentionally arousing emotion in an audience.

This is manipulative and a form of communication.

A similar arousal can be the result of expression.
Such expression denotes and belongs to an individual.
It is actually a characteristic of individuals.
It isn't a form of communication although observers are often mistaken.

Emotion and exhibiting symptoms of emotion are different.
The former is necessary for art and is a personal reaction to a stimulus.
Symptoms of emotion are what an observer sees.
There may be manipulation of those symbols without any emotion at all (actor).

The relationship between an artist and the work is thus a personal one.
It's linked to the inner state of the artist prior to, and during creating.
That may ultimately be a work of art.

It doesn't really matter what you do at the start.
The most important thing is to actually do something.
Let's see what happens here when I do this?

Random starts do not necessarily have to be the case.
You can plan your starts.
But take your time.
Don't rush enjoy the experience and see what you can find out.

Once you begin, you can alter or change what you have done.
It's better to do something and be wrong, than do nothing.
Mistakes can be corrected, and you learn what not to do at the same time.
Any experiment does not even have to be finished!

In the process you'll discover whatever you find out.
More importantly the discoveries are yours.
They're part of your actual experience rather than just following instructions.

Your knowledge grows from your own experiences.
This is what real learning is about.
Your experience and confidence grows for the more you do the better you get!

You are the judge of quality, which is a variable that changes over time.
Old works you thought were excellent at the time done are they now?

There are three ways to transition from experimenting to being an artist.
Once you have done the hard yards this is an easy and natural step.

The first follows the REALISM path.
This continues from the previous pattern of experiments.
The focus is on photographs and pictures to a continuing search for reality.
The second pathway is based on OBSERVATION.
This is a more traditional but a foundation was laid with the MMM experiments.

The third pathway is linked to your IMAGINATION.
This focus is more personal but again a foundation from MMM experiments.

Perhaps you want to try them all?
Then follow a sequence of MMM experiments outlined fora logical progression.

Only two pathways are possible if your MMM focus is NOT observable.
Follow either / or both of the Realism and Imagination pathways.
You could follow just one of the pathways?

What if your particular MMM focus is not one of those template Groups!
That's not really a problem - select the one that's closest.
For example if your focus is on fairies choose the People Group.
Then substitute fairies for people when creating your MMM experiments.

But your focus is quite different – say World War 1 military aircraft?
There's no group anything like that.
Just select a group and substitute your focus for whatever is already there.

Your MMM experiments are like the athletes training program.
Like an Olympic athlete to remain at the highest level you keep training.
Your MMM experiments become a normal routine.
So you need to construct YOUR OWN MMM experimental programs.

Then training never stops.
Perhaps start each day with a short period of experiments.
Then move to your main artistic tasks.

By actually painting you understand how to do what you want to!
There's no other way.

You learn by doing.
You do not learn by someone telling you what to do.
Then you only learn they know what to do and if you get stuck you ask them.

By now you should have an experimental attitude.
You are scientific about your art learning so set yourself challenges.
See what happens here when you do this?

Magic Multiple Miniature experiments can be copied several times.
Then you can compare different experiments with the same image.
This highlights learning that would otherwise take much longer.

Use ONE MMM experiment as a template for a series of explorations.
Use the same materials in different combinations (black, grays, white).
Use different materials entirely (pencil, felt pen).

Select DIFFERENT MMM experiments as for a series of explorations.
Use the same element combinations (black, grays) on each one.

Use the same materials each time (pencil, felt pen, paint).

Explore further according to your curiosity.
For example an MMM experiment could be printed on gray or coloured paper.
You could even distort the MMM image!

Don't worry about whether you are doing the experiments correctly.
Do something it's certain to be right and you discover what you find out.

Once you begin, you can alter or change what you have done.
It's better to do something and be wrong, than do nothing.
Mistakes can be corrected, and you learn what not to do at the same time.

An experiment does not even have to be finished!
Your knowledge grows from your own experience which is real learning.

Most importantly any discoveries are yours.
They're part of your actual experience rather than just following instructions.
Your experience and confidence grow for the more you do the better you'll get!

Random starts do not necessarily have to be the case.
You can plan your starts but take your time.
Don't rush enjoy the experience and see what you can find out.

1. NOW START: PORTRAITS.

FIRST Experience Unit:

UNIT 1: Experiment 1
Copy or photocopy or print a black and white MMM image you have chosen.
Materials:
Your choice of non-paint, opaque or transparent paint (black and white).
Brush (if using paint).
Begin:
Paint the MMM image in black and white.
Match the original tones.
Notice the shapes in the portrait.
Conclude Clean up.

UNIT 1: Experiment 2
Copy, photocopy or print out a black and white MMM image you have chosen.
Materials:
Your choice of non-paint, opaque or transparent paint.
Brush (if using paint), white paper (small).
Begin:
Copy the portrait from your MMM image.
Preliminary drawing in thin paint.
Establish overall shape of the portrait.
Keep the painting broad.
Then:
Use a bigger brush with black and white
Notice the shape of the portrait.
Conclude: Clean up.

UNIT 1: Experiment 3

Copy photocopy or print out a black and white MMM image you have chosen.

Materials:

Your choice of non-paint, opaque or transparent paint (black and white).

Large brush (if using paint), white paper (small).

Begin:

Copy the portrait from your MMM image.

Preliminary drawing in thin paint.

Establish overall shape of the portrait.

Keep the painting broad.

Then:

Use a bigger brush with black and white

Change from the original tones.

Notice the shape of the portrait.

Conclude:

Clean up.

UNIT 1: Experiment 4

Copy or photocopy or print out a coloured MMM image you have chosen.

Materials:

Your choice of non-paint, opaque or transparent paint (black and white).

Large brush (if using paint), white paper (small).

Begin:

Copy the portrait from your MMM image.

Preliminary drawing in thin paint with brush.

Block in darkest and lightest areas with thin paint.

Establish overall shape of the portrait keeping the painting simple and broad.

Check the relationships between the different areas.

Establish positions of eyes, nose, mouth, chin relative to each other.

Then:

Use a bigger brush with black and white

Copy the original tones.

Conclude:

Clean up.

UNIT 1: Experiment 5

Copy or photocopy or print out a coloured MMM image you have chosen.

Materials:

Your choice of non-paint, opaque or transparent paint (dark and light).

Large brush (if using paint), white paper (small).

Begin:

Copy the portrait from your MMM image.

Preliminary drawing in thin paint with brush.

Block in darkest and lightest areas with thin paint.

Establish overall shape of the portrait.

Keep the painting simple and broad.

Check the relationships between the different areas.

Establish positions of eyes, nose, mouth, chin relative to each other.

Then:

Use a bigger brush with dark and light paint

Copy the original tones.

Conclude: Clean up.

UNIT 1: Experiment 6

Copy or photocopy or print out a coloured MMM image you have chosen.

Materials:

Your choice of non-paint, opaque or transparent paint (dark and light).

Large brush (if using paint), toned or coloured paper (small).

Begin:

Copy the portrait from your MMM image.

Preliminary drawing in thin paint with brush.

Block in darkest and lightest areas with thin paint.

Establish overall shape of the portrait keeping the painting simple and broad.

Check the relationships between the different areas.

Establish positions of eyes, nose, mouth, chin relative to each other.

Then:

Use a bigger brush with dark and light paint

Copy the original tones.

Conclude: Clean up.

Further thoughts:

Copy other images of portraits.

Use dark and light paint (or non-paint).

Establish overall shape of the portrait.

Keep the painting simple and broad.

Check the relationships between the different areas.

Establish positions of eyes, nose, mouth, chin relative to each other.

Note the spaces in between these areas.

SECOND Experience Unit:

UNIT 2: Experiment 1

Modify copy or photocopy or print a specific MMM image you have chosen in colour.

Materials:

Your choice of non-paint, opaque or transparent paint (dark and light).

Large brush (if using paint), toned or coloured paper (small).

Begin:

Copy an portrait from your MMM image.

Preliminary drawing in thin paint with brush.

Block in darkest and lightest areas with thin paint.

Establish overall shape of the portrait.

Keep the painting simple and broad.

Check the relationships between the different areas.

Establish positions of eyes, nose, mouth, chin relative to each other.

Then:

Use a bigger brush with dark and light paint

Copy the original tones.

Conclude:

Clean up.

UNIT 2: Experiment 2

A specific coloured MMM image if possible taken by you.

Materials:

Choose non-paint, opaque or transparent paint (dark and light + a local colour).

Local colour is the approximate colour of things (black cat, brown dog).

Large brush (if using paint), white paper (small).

Begin:

Copy portrait from your MMM image.

Preliminary drawing in thin paint with brush.

Block in darkest and lightest areas with thin paint.

Establish overall shape of the portrait.

Keep the painting simple and broad.

Check the relationships between the different areas.

Establish positions of eyes, nose, mouth, chin relative to each other.

Then:

Use a bigger brush with dark and light paint to show the original tones.

Use more dark and light paint to show shape and shape.

Use the other colour to add local (as in the portrait) colour.

This only needs to approximate the portrait colour.

Do NOT overwork the experiment.

Many details you know are there may not be shown.

Conclude:

Clean up.

UNIT 2: Experiment 3

Coloured MMM image used in the previous experiment.

Materials:

Choose non-paint, opaque or transparent paint (dark and light + a local colour).

Large brush (if using paint), white paper (small).

Begin:

Copy portrait from your MMM image.

Preliminary drawing in thin paint with brush.

Block in darkest and lightest areas with thin paint.

Establish overall shape of the portrait.

Keep the painting simple and broad.

Check the relationships between the different areas.

Establish positions of eyes, nose, mouth, chin relative to each other.

Note the spaces in between.

Then:

Use dark and light paint to show the original tones.

Use more dark and light paint to show shape and shape.

Add local (as in the portrait) colour.

This only needs to approximate the portrait colour.

Do NOT overwork the experiment.

Many details you know are there may not be shown.

Conclude:

Clean up.

UNIT 2: Experiment 4

Coloured MMM image used in the previous experiment.

Materials:

Choose non-paint, opaque or transparent paint (dark and light + a local colour).

Large brush (if using paint), white toned or coloured paper (small).

Begin:

Copy portrait from your MMM image.

Preliminary drawing in thin paint with brush.

Block in darkest and lightest areas with thin paint.

Establish overall shape of the portrait keeping the painting simple and broad.

Check the relationships between the different areas.

Establish positions of eyes, nose, mouth, chin relative to each other.

Note the spaces in between.

Then:

Use dark and light paint to show the original tones.

Use more dark and light paint to show shape and shape.

Add local (as in the portrait) colour although this only needs to approximate the portrait colour.

Develop your experiment but do NOT overwork it.

Gradually modify the tones and colours.

Many details may not be shown.

Conclude:

Clean up.

UNIT 2: Experiment 5

Coloured MMM image used in the previous experiment.

Materials:

Choose non-paint, opaque or transparent paint (dark and light + a warm and cool colour).

Two brushes (if using paint), white toned or coloured paper (a little larger).

Begin:

Copy portrait from your MMM image.

Preliminary drawing in thin paint with brush.

Block in darkest and lightest areas with thin paint.

Establish overall shape of the portrait.

Keep the painting simple and broad.

Check the relationships between the different areas.

Establish positions of eyes, nose, mouth, chin relative to each other - note the spaces in between.

Then:

Use dark and light paint to show the original tones.

Add more dark and light to show other shape and shapes.

Add local (as in the portrait) colour.

This only needs to approximate the portrait colour.

Develop your experiment but do NOT overwork it.

Gradually modify the tones and colours.

Use warm and cool colours to show depth.

Many details may not be shown.

Conclude:

Clean up.

UNIT 2: Experiment 6

Coloured MMM image used in the previous experiment.

Materials:

Choose-paint, opaque or transparent paint (dark and light + a warm and cool colour).

Two brushes (if using paint), white toned or coloured paper (a little larger).

Begin:

Copy portrait from your MMM image.

Preliminary drawing in thin paint with brush.

Block in darkest and lightest areas with thin paint.

Establish overall shape of the portrait.

Keep the painting simple and broad.

Check the relationships between the different areas.

Establish positions of eyes, nose, mouth, chin relative to each other - note the spaces in between.

Then:

Use dark and light paint to show the original tones - more dark and light to show shape and shape.

Add local (as in the portrait) colour.

This only needs to approximate the portrait colour.

Develop your experiment but do NOT overwork it - many details may not be shown.

Gradually modify the tones and colours.

Use warm and cool colours to show depth.

Conclude:

Clean up.

Further thoughts:

Use other photographs you have taken to explore other views.

THIRD Experience Unit:

UNIT 3: Experiment 1
Modify copy photocopy or print out a specific coloured MMM image from memory.

Materials:
Your choice of non-paint, opaque or transparent paint (dark and light also is warm and cool).
A brush (if using paint), white toned or coloured paper (a little larger).

Begin:
Copy portrait from your MMM image in dark and light areas with thin paint.
Match original tones.
Use the dark and light colours to show portrait shape.
Use warm and cool colour to show depth.
Check the relationships between the different areas.
Establish positions of eyes, nose, mouth, chin relative to each other.
Note the spaces in between.

Then:
Add local (as in the portrait) colour.
This only needs to approximate the portrait colour.
Develop your experiment but do NOT overwork it.
Gradually modify the tones and colours.

Conclude:
Clean up.

UNIT 3: Experiment 2

Memory of a specific coloured MMM image if possible taken by yourself.

Materials:

Your choice of non-paint, opaque or transparent paint (dark, light also warm / cool + local colour).

Two brushes (if using paint), white toned or coloured paper (a little larger).

A piece of glass.

Begin:

Trace portrait image onto glass.

Copy portrait from your glass tracing in dark and light areas with thin paint.

Match original tones.

Use the dark and light colours to show portrait shape.

Use warm and cool colour to show depth.

Check the relationships between the different areas.

Establish positions of eyes, nose, mouth, chin relative to each other.

Note the spaces in between.

Then:

Add local (as in the portrait) colour.

This only needs to approximate the portrait colour.

Develop your experiment but do NOT overwork it.

Gradually modify the tones and colours.

Conclude:

Clean up.

UNIT 3: Experiment 3

Memory of a specific coloured MMM image used in the previous experiment.

Materials:

Your choice of non-paint, opaque or transparent paint (dark, light also warm / cool + local colour).

Two brushes (if using paint), white toned or coloured paper (a little larger).

A tracing glass.

Begin:

Trace portrait image onto glass.

Copy portrait from your glass tracing in dark and light areas with thin paint.

Match original tones.

Check the relationships between the different areas.

Establish positions of eyes, nose, mouth, chin relative to each other.

Note the spaces in between.

Then:

Use the dark and light colours but vary from the original tones.

Use the dark and light colours to show portrait shape.

Add local (as in the portrait) colour.

This only needs to approximate the portrait colour.

Develop your experiment but do NOT overwork it.

Gradually modify the tones and colours.

Use warm and cool colour to show depth.

Conclude:

Clean up.

UNIT 3: Experiment 4

Memory of a specific coloured MMM image used in the previous experiment.

Materials:

Your choice of non-paint, opaque or transparent paint (dark, light also warm / cool + local colour).

Two brushes (if using paint), white toned or coloured paper (a little larger).

A tracing glass.

Begin:

Trace portrait image onto glass.

Copy portrait from your glass tracing in dark and light areas with thin paint.

Match original tones.

Check the relationships between the different areas.

Establish positions of eyes, nose, mouth, chin relative to each other.

Note the spaces in between.

Then:

Use the dark and light colours but vary from the original tones.

Use the dark and light colours to show portrait shape.

Add local (as in the portrait) colour which only needs to approximate the portrait colour.

Develop your experiment but do NOT overwork it.

Gradually modify the tones and colours and using warm and cool colour to show depth.

Do not attempt too much detail - only paint what can be seen by a viewer.

Conclude:

Clean up.

UNIT 3: Experiment 5

Memory of a specific coloured MMM image used in the previous experiment.

Materials:

Your choice of non-paint, opaque or transparent paint (dark, light also warm / cool + local colour).

Two brushes (if using paint), white toned or coloured paper (a little larger).

A tracing glass.

Begin:

Trace portrait image onto glass.

Copy portrait from your glass tracing in dark and light areas with thin paint.

Match original tones.

Check the relationships between the different areas.

Establish positions of eyes, nose, mouth, chin relative to each other.

Note the spaces in between.

Then:

Use the dark and light colours but vary from the original tones.

Use the dark and light colours to show portrait shape.

Add local (as in the portrait) colour.

This only needs to approximate the portrait colour.

Develop your experiment but do NOT overwork it.

Gradually modify the tones and colours.

Use soft and hard edges for modelling.

Boundaries between shapes should not always be too sharp or clear cut.

A soft irregular transition is required from time to time.

Gradually modify tones and colours – for example use warm and cool colour to show depth.

Suggest texture by dry-brush or sgraffito techniques.

Thicker paint may be required to do that.

Do not attempt too much detail - only paint what can be seen by a viewer.

Conclude:

Clean up.

UNIT3: Experiment 6

Memory of a specific coloured MMM image used in the previous experiment.

Materials:

Your choice of non-paint, opaque or transparent paint (dark, light also warm / cool + local colour).

Two brushes (if using paint), white toned or coloured paper (a little larger).

A tracing glass.

Begin:

Trace portrait image onto glass.

Copy portrait from your glass tracing in dark and light areas with thin paint.

Match original tones.

Check the relationships between the different areas.

Establish positions of eyes, nose, mouth, chin relative to each other.

Note the spaces in between.

Then:

Use the dark and light colours but vary from the original tones.

Use the dark and light colours to show portrait shape.

Add local (as in the portrait) colour which only needs to approximate the portrait colour.

Develop your experiment but do NOT overwork it.

Gradually modify the tones and colours.

Use soft and hard edges for modelling.

Boundaries between shapes should not always be too sharp or clear cut.

A soft irregular transition is required from time to time.

Gradually modify tones and colours – for example use warm and cool colour to show depth.

Suggest texture by dry-brush or sgraffito techniques.

Thicker paint may be required to do that.

Do not attempt too much detail - only paint what can be seen by a viewer.

Conclude:

Clean up.

Further thoughts:

Use memories of other photographs you have taken to explore other views.

DEVELOPMENT: Extensions

In the Development extension activities:

Draw on what you have learnt.

You can link what you have learned to your own goals.

DEVELOPMENT: Extension 1

Copy or photocopy or print out the MMM image you have chosen.

Materials:

Use the SAME materials as used in a previous experiment from Unit One.

Use the SAME MMM image as used in a previous experiment Unit One.

Begin:

BUT repeat only one of the experiments.

DEVELOPMENT: Extension 2

Modify copy or photocopy or print out of the MMM image you have chosen.

Materials:

Use the SAME materials as used in a previous experiment from Unit Two.

Use the SAME MMM image as used in a previous experiment Unit Two.

Begin:

BUT repeat only one of the experiments.

DEVELOPMENT: Extension 3

Modify copy or photocopy or print of the MMM image you have chosen from memory.

Materials:

Use the SAME materials as used in a previous experiment from Unit Three.

Use the SAME MMM image as used in a previous experiment Unit Three.

Begin:

BUT repeat only one of the experiments.

CONGRATULATIONS.

You have taken the REALISM pathway.
This continues from the previous pattern of experiments.
Focus on photographs and pictures as a way to a continuing search for reality.
This could be the final step to being the artist you want to be.

But perhaps you want to try them all?
Then follow the sequence of MMM experiments as outlined.
There is a logical progression.

The second pathway is based on OBSERVATION.
This focus is a more traditional approach.
But the foundation has been laid with the MMM experiments.

But if your MMM focus is NOT observable this pathway is not for you.
Then you can go straight to the third pathway.

The third pathway is linked to your IMAGINATION.
This focus is more personal.
But again there is a foundation from the MMM experiments.

Your MMM experiments are like the athletes training program.
But the training never stops.
Olympic athletes want to remain at the highest level they must keep training.
Similarly your MMM experiments become a normal routine.

Make notes, do sketches and record what you can see.
This is material you can draw on when continuing your MMM experiments.
Make a habit to carry a small sketchpad or scraps of paper and a pen or pencil.

Perhaps start each day with a short period of experiments.
Then move to your main artistic tasks.

You'll need to construct YOUR OWN MMM experimental programs.
By now this should not be difficult.

Planning major works could follow from that.
But do them as extensions of your MMM experiments.
A slightly larger experiment can develop into a major work.
Then much of the planning and preparatory work has been done.

2. OBSERVED PORTRAITS.

Continue with the subject matter you want to paint really well.
Your focus is always on portraits.

Like the Californian artist focus on one (child, mother).
Then even from the start you can become a specialist.
You will also focus on something you are interested in.
This will help maintain the necessary motivation while you learn.

But now observe your chosen painting focus.
This means you are limited to things you can actually look at.

Get to understand your subjects.
Over time you will develop the individual paining skills needed.
You will also know how to paint your portraits your way.

Move from a general focus to a narrower one.
So you focus on academics, musicians, children or old people.
You'll note the similarities and also the differences.
Because they are all people you will learn much quicker.

You could progress from portraits to head and shoulders to full figures.
Follow this pattern for long enough, and you'll be able to paint anything!

Make notes, do sketches and record what you can see.
This is material you can draw on when continuing your MMM experiments.
Carry a small sketchpad or even scraps of paper and a pen or pencil.

Set up MMM experiments right where your observation focus is.
The Impressionists popularized painting outdoors.
A still life arrangement is an alternative.
Most portraits are posed.

Your observation helps you understand your individual.
Over time you will develop the paining skills needed.
You will also know how to paint your subject your way.

Eventually you can focus on another subject.
If it is related to your original theme you will learn much quicker.
From one kind of person to another.

People who do things well also do them faster than those who don't.
That applies to painting just as much as anything else.
It's one of the indicators of skill.

You should have noticed that repetition helps your skill development.
Skill in art, sport or even medicine is basically the same phenomenon.
It's practiced behaviour in action.
Most artists don't do anywhere near enough to develop real skill.

Work a number of experiments at the same time increases productivity.
For you reduce wasted time.
If you run into a dead-end with one painting move to another for a fresh start.
When the initial painting is returned to, there will be a different attitude.
Otherwise set it aside again.
Usually you'll find most works will finish fresh and roughly about the same time.

Working on a number of paintings at the same time also saves materials.
A particular colour can be applied to the experiment for which it was intended.
BUT there are bound to be others where that same colour will be appropriate.
When you buy paint, buy in quantity, but only use as needed.

Avoid major works.
They take time (years), usually done slowly and are often large and complex.

You'll tend to labour over them as you try to do your best.
Instead occasionally do a slightly larger experiment.

Focus on learning what you can.
Action with materials = technique.
Practiced techniques = skill.
Habitual technique + skill = style.

Do you have a sketchbook?
You are probably familiar with a sketchbook.
It can be an old book, as long as you can write, scribble, draw, or make notes.
It doesn't really matter whether it has lines or the pages are blank.

It'll end up with your ideas, or memory aids for your ideas in most cases.
Naturally ideas for paintings will be there.
Writing down thoughts is a powerful way to commit them to your memory bank.
Then they are accessible later.
Look at various pages in your sketchbook a later date will refresh those ideas.
That will go beyond what is merely recorded in your book.
Writing ideas down you build a bridge from what you see and action you take.

Your Ideas sketchbook can be where you start your planning.
Sometimes this will be repetitive, as minor variations are tested.
But they have to be worked through to find out what happens.
Effective planning is the beginnings of effective actions.
Your plans are the test runs for the real world.
Plans don't make anything happen, but they certainly ease the way.

How will you get the most from your sketchbook?

You'll always get more from what you draw or write than what you read or hear.

Do sensible ideas there is a chance that you'll improve on your past efforts.

If you do not try anything then there is no chance of an improvement at all.

This is particularly useful when you are observing fleeting moments.

Sometimes they'll turn out great, but at other times not so.

No need to be brave for there's no risk do enough fleeting experiments.

They'll improve and you'll be able to capture paint passing moments of life.

They'll have spontaneity often lacking in a photographic based artwork.

NOW START: OBSERVED PORTRAITS

FIRST Experience Unit:

UNIT 1: Experiment 1

Start with an MMM portrait observation.

Materials:

Your choice of (dark, light also warm / cool) non-paint, opaque or transparent paint.

Two brushes (if using paint), white toned or coloured paper (a little larger).

Begin:

Copy portrait from your MMM observation.

Use thin paint (large brush) and only show what is necessary.

Then:

Use the dark and light colours to show portrait shape and paint smaller parts later.

Use soft and hard edges for modelling - boundaries should not always be too sharp or clear cut.

A soft irregular transition is required from time to time.

Develop your experiment but do NOT overwork it.

Gradually modify tones and colours – for example use warm and cool colour to show depth.

Suggest texture by dry-brush or sgraffito techniques. – may need thicker paint to do that.

Conclude:

Clean up.

UNIT 1: Experiment 2

Start with the same MMM portrait observation as in the previous experiment.

Materials:

Your choice of (dark, light - warm / cool + another colour) non-paint, opaque or transparent paint.

Two brushes (if using paint), white toned or coloured paper (a little larger).

Begin:

Copy one part of the portrait from your MMM observation (head, eyes, ears).

Use thin paint (large brush).

Only show what is necessary.

Then:

Use the dark and light colours to show portrait shape.

Use thin paint before using thick paint.

Paint smaller parts later.

Use soft and hard edges for modelling the shape.

Boundaries between shapes should not always be too sharp or clear cut.

A soft irregular transition is required from time to time.

Develop your experiment but do NOT overwork it.

Gradually modify tones and colours – for example use warm and cool colour to show depth.

Suggest texture by dry-brush or sgraffito techniques.

Thicker paint may be required to do that.

Do not attempt too much detail - only paint what can be seen by a viewer.

Conclude:

Clean up.

UNIT 1: Experiment 3

Start with the same MMM portrait observation as in the previous experiment.

Materials:

Your choice of (dark, light - warm / cool + another colour) non-paint, opaque or transparent paint.

Two brushes (if using paint), white toned or coloured paper (a little larger).

Begin:

Copy same part of the portrait from your MMM observation (head, eyes, ears).

Use thin paint (large brush) and only show what is necessary.

Then:

Use the dark and light colours to show portrait shape.

Use thin paint before using thick paint.

Paint unimportant areas before important parts and paint smaller parts later.

Use soft and hard edges for modelling - boundaries should not always be too sharp or clear cut.

A soft irregular transition is required from time to time.

Develop your experiment but do NOT overwork it.

Gradually modify tones and colours – for example use warm and cool colour to show depth.

Suggest texture by dry-brush or sgraffito techniques.

Thicker paint may be required to do that.

Do not attempt too much detail - only paint what can be seen by a viewer.

Conclude:

Clean up.

UNIT 1: Experiment 4

Start with a different MMM portrait observation.

Materials:

Your choice of (dark, light - warm / cool + another colour) non-paint, opaque or transparent paint.

Two brushes (if using paint), white toned or coloured paper (a little larger).

Begin:

Copy same part of the portrait from your MMM observation (head, eyes, ears).

Use thin paint (large brush) and only show what is necessary.

Then:

Use the dark and light colours to show portrait shape.

Use thin paint before using thick paint.

Paint unimportant areas before important parts.

Paint smaller parts later.

Use soft and hard edges for modelling the shape.

Develop your experiment but do NOT overwork it.

Gradually modify tones and colours – for example use warm and cool colour to show depth.

Suggest texture by dry-brush or sgraffito techniques – may require thicker paint.

Do not attempt too much detail - only paint what can be seen by a viewer.

Conclude:

Clean up.

UNIT 1: Experiment 5

Start with a different MMM portrait observation.

Materials:

Your choice of (dark, light - warm / cool + another colour) non-paint, opaque or transparent paint.

Two brushes (if using paint), white toned or coloured paper (a little larger).

Begin:

Copy same part of the portrait from your MMM observation (head, eyes, ears).

Include an extra component (environment)

Use thin paint (large brush) and only show what is necessary.

Then:

Note the direction of the light.

Use the dark and light colours to show portrait shape.

At the same time establish the light source.

Paint unimportant areas before important parts.

Paint the background to establish brightness of the painting (light/dark).

Use thin paint before using thick paint.

Paint smaller parts later.

Use soft and hard edges for modelling the shape.

Develop your experiment but do NOT overwork it.

Gradually modify tones and colours – for example use warm and cool colour to show depth.

Suggest texture by dry-brush or sgraffito techniques – may require thicker paint.

Do not attempt too much detail - only paint what can be seen by a viewer.

Conclude:

Clean up.

UNIT 1: Experiment 6

Start with a different MMM portrait observation.

Materials:

Your choice of (dark, light - warm / cool + another colour) non-paint, opaque or transparent paint.

Two brushes (if using paint), white toned or coloured paper (a little larger).

Begin:

Copy same part of the portrait from your MMM observation (head, eyes, ears).

Include an extra component (environment)

Use thin paint (large brush) and only show what is necessary.

Then:

Note the direction of the light.

Use the dark and light colours to show portrait shape.

At the same time establish the light source.

Paint unimportant areas before important parts.

Paint the background to establish brightness of the painting (light/dark).

Use thin paint before using thick paint.

Paint smaller parts later.

Use soft and hard edges for modelling the shape.

Develop your experiment but do NOT overwork it.

Gradually modify tones and colours – for example use warm and cool colour to show depth.

Suggest texture by dry-brush or sgraffito techniques – may require thicker paint.

Do not attempt too much detail - only paint what can be seen by a viewer.

Conclude:

Clean up.

Further thoughts:

Use other observations of your own to explore other views.

Suggest portrait shape by painting background first.

Paint a portrait with as few brushstrokes as possible.

SECOND Experience Unit:

UNIT 2: Experiment 1

Start based on an MMM portrait observation you have made.

Materials:

Your choice of (dark, light - warm / cool + another colour) non-paint, opaque or transparent paint.

Two brushes (if using paint), white toned or coloured paper (a little larger).

Begin:

Copy a different part of the portrait from your MMM observation (head, eye, ears).

Include an extra component (dish, kennel, environment)

Paint the background to establish brightness of the painting (light/dark).

Use thin paint (large brush) and only show what is necessary.

Then:

Establish a single source for the light.

Use the dark and light colours to show portrait shape.

Use thin paint before using thick paint.

Paint unimportant areas before important parts.

Paint smaller parts later.

Use soft and hard edges for modelling the shape.

Develop your experiment but do NOT overwork it.

Gradually modify tones and colours – for example use warm and cool colour to show depth.

Suggest texture by dry-brush or sgraffito techniques.

Under-paint area before laying on thicker paint.

Conclude:

Clean up.

UNIT 2: Experiment 2

Base start on a different MMM portrait observation used in the previous experiment.

Materials:

Your choice of (dark, light - warm / cool + portrait colour) non-paint, opaque or transparent paint.

Two brushes (if using paint), white toned or coloured paper (a little larger).

Begin:

Copy same part of the portrait from your MMM observation (head, eye, ears).

Use thin paint (large brush) and only show what is necessary.

Include an extra component (dish, kennel, environment)

Paint the background to establish brightness of the painting (light/dark).

Then:

Establish a single source for the light and use the dark and light colours to show portrait shape.

Use thin paint before using thick paint.

Paint unimportant areas before important parts - paint smaller parts later.

Use soft and hard edges for modelling the shape.

Develop your experiment but do NOT overwork it.

Gradually modify tones and colours – for example use warm and cool colour to show depth.

Suggest texture by dry-brush or sgraffito techniques.

Under-paint area before laying on thicker paint.

Conclude:

Clean up.

UNIT 2: Experiment 3

Base start on a different MMM portrait observation used in the previous experiment.

Materials:

Your choice of (dark, light - warm / cool + portrait colour) non-paint, opaque or transparent paint.

Two brushes (if using paint), white toned or coloured paper (a little larger).

Begin:

Copy same part of the portrait from your MMM observation (head, eye, ears).

Use thin paint (large brush) and only show what is necessary.

Include an extra component (dish, kennel, environment)

Paint the background to establish brightness of the painting (light/dark).

Then:

Establish direction of the light.

Use the dark and light colours to show portrait shape.

Use thin paint before using thick paint.

Paint unimportant areas before important parts.

Work from most distant to closest areas.

Paint smaller parts later.

Use soft and hard edges for modelling the shape.

Develop your experiment but do NOT overwork it.

Gradually modify tones and colours – for example use warm and cool colour to show depth.

Suggest texture by dry-brush or sgraffito techniques and under-paint beforehand.

Conclude:

Clean up.

UNIT 2: Experiment 4

Base start on a different MMM portrait observation used in the previous experiment.

Materials:

Your choice of (dark, light - warm / cool + portrait colour) non-paint, opaque or transparent paint.

Two brushes (if using paint), white toned or coloured paper (a little larger).

Begin:

Copy same part of the portrait from your MMM observation (head, eye, ears).

Use thin paint (large brush) and only show what is necessary.

Include an extra component (dish, kennel, environment)

Paint the background to establish brightness of the painting (light/dark).

Then:

Establish direction of the light then use the dark and light colours to show portrait shape.

Use thin paint before using thick paint.

Paint unimportant areas before important parts.

Work from most distant to closest areas - paint smaller parts later.

Use soft and hard edges for modelling the shape.

Develop your experiment but do NOT overwork it.

Gradually modify tones and colours – for example use warm and cool colour to show depth.

Suggest texture by dry-brush or sgraffito techniques and under-paint beforehand.

Conclude:

Clean up.

UNIT 2: Experiment 5

Base start on a different MMM portrait observation used in the previous experiment.

Materials:

Your choice of (dark, light - warm / cool + portrait colour) non-paint, opaque or transparent paint.

Two brushes (if using paint), white toned or coloured paper (a little larger).

Begin:

Copy same part of the portrait from your MMM observation (head, eye, ears).

Use thin paint (large brush) and only show what is necessary.

Include an extra component (dish, kennel, environment)

Paint the background to establish brightness of the painting (light/dark).

Then:

Establish direction of the light then use the dark and light colours to show portrait shape.

Use thin paint before using thick paint.

Paint unimportant areas before important parts.

Work from most distant to closest areas.

Paint smaller parts later.

Use soft and hard edges for modelling the shape.

Develop your experiment but do NOT overwork it.

Gradually modify tones and colours – using cool before warm to show depth.

Suggest texture by dry-brush or sgraffito techniques and under-paint beforehand.

Conclude:

Clean up.

UNIT 2: Experiment 6

Base start on a different MMM portrait observation used in the previous experiment.

Materials:

Your choice of (dark, light - warm / cool + portrait colour) non-paint, opaque or transparent paint.

Two brushes (if using paint), white toned or coloured paper (a little larger).

Begin:

Copy same part of the portrait from your MMM observation (head, eye, ears).

Use thin paint (large brush) and only show what is necessary.

Include an extra component (dish, kennel, environment)

Paint the background to establish brightness of the painting (light/dark).

Then:

Establish direction of the light then use the dark and light colours to show portrait shape.

Use thin paint before using thick paint.

Paint unimportant areas before important parts.

Work from most distant to closest areas.

Paint smaller parts later.

Use soft and hard edges for modelling the shape.

Develop your experiment but do NOT overwork it.

Gradually modify tones and colours – using cool before warm to show depth.

Suggest texture by dry-brush or sgraffito techniques and under-paint beforehand.

Conclude:

Clean up.

Further thoughts:

Paint portrait silhouettes.

Paint background to suggest shape of portrait.

Paint a portrait with as few brushstrokes as possible.

Use a spotlight to experiment with different sources and directions of lighting.

THIRD Experience Unit:

UNIT 3: Experiment 1

Start based on two different MMM portrait observations you have made.

Materials:

Your choice of (dark, light - warm / cool + portrait colour) non-paint, opaque or transparent paint.

Two brushes (if using paint), white toned or coloured paper (a little larger).

Begin:

Copy the same part of each portrait from your MMM observations (head, eye, ears).

Use thin paint (large brush) and only show what is necessary.

Paint the background to establish brightness of the painting (light/dark).

Then:

Establish direction of the light then use the dark and light colours to show portrait shape.

Use thin paint before using thick paint.

Paint unimportant areas before important parts.

Use larger brush for larger areas and paint smaller parts later.

Work from most distant to closest areas.

Use soft and hard edges for modelling the shape.

Decide the dominant colours.

Develop your experiment but do NOT overwork it.

Gradually modify tones and colours – using cool before warm to show depth.

Suggest texture by dry-brush or sgraffito techniques and under-paint beforehand.

Conclude:

Clean up.

UNIT 3: Experiment 2

Start based on two different MMM portrait observations you have made.

Materials:

Your choice of (dark, light - warm / cool + portrait colour) non-paint, opaque or transparent paint.

Two brushes (if using paint), white toned or coloured paper (a little larger).

Begin:

Copy the same part of each portrait from your MMM observations (head, eye, ears).

Establish direction of the light then use the dark and light colours to show portrait shape.

Use thin paint (large brush) and only show what is necessary.

Paint unimportant areas before important parts.

Paint the background to establish brightness of the painting (light/dark).

Use larger brush for larger areas and paint smaller parts later - thin paint before using thick paint.

Decide the dominant colours and under-paint accordingly.

Suggest texture by dry-brush or sgraffito techniques and under-paint beforehand.

Then:

Work from most distant to closest areas.

Use soft and hard edges for modelling the shape.

Boundary between shapes isn't always sharp or precise.

Develop your experiment but do NOT overwork it.

Gradually modify tones and colours – using cool before warm to show depth.

Conclude:

Clean up.

UNIT 3: Experiment 3

Start based on two different MMM portrait observations you have made.

Materials:

Your choice of (dark, light - warm / cool + portrait colour) non-paint, opaque or transparent paint.

Two brushes (if using paint), white toned or coloured paper (a little larger).

Begin:

Copy a different part of the portrait from each MMM observation (head, eye, ears).

Copy the same part for each portrait - note light source.

Paint unimportant areas before important parts.

Use thin paint (large brush) and only show what is necessary.

Use larger brush for larger areas and paint smaller parts later - thin paint before using thick paint.

Decide the dominant colours and under-paint accordingly.

Suggest texture by dry-brush or sgraffito techniques and under-paint beforehand.

Then:

Note direction of the light and keep it consistent through the experiment.

Paint the background to establish brightness of the painting (light/dark).

Paint dark and light areas to show the shape of the portrait.

Use soft and hard edges for modelling the shape.

Work from most distant to closest areas.

Boundary between shapes isn't always sharp or precise.

Develop your experiment but do NOT overwork it.

Gradually modify tones and colours – using cool before warm to show depth.

Conclude:

Clean up.

UNIT 3: Experiment 4

Start based on three different MMM portrait observations you have made.

Materials:

Your choice of (dark, light - warm / cool + portrait colour) non-paint, opaque or transparent paint.

Two brushes (if using paint), white toned or coloured paper (a little larger).

Begin:

Copy same part of the portrait as previously from the MMM observations (head, eye, ears).

Blend the two MMM portrait observation memories.

Plan the light source to unify the two portrait images.

Paint unimportant areas before important parts.

Thin paint (large brush) only show what is necessary - larger areas and paint smaller parts later.

Use thin paint before using thick paint.

Decide the dominant colours and under-paint accordingly.

Suggest texture by dry-brush or sgraffito techniques and under-paint beforehand.

Then:

Note direction of the light and keep it consistent through the experiment.

Paint the background to establish brightness of the painting (light/dark).

Paint dark and light areas to show the shape of the portrait.

Use soft and hard edges for modelling the shape.

Work from most distant to closest areas.

Boundary between shapes isn't always sharp or precise.

Develop your experiment but do NOT overwork it.

Gradually modify tones and colours – using cool before warm to show depth.

Conclude:

Clean up.

UNIT 3: Experiment 5

Start based on another different MMM portrait observation you have made.

Materials:

Your choice of (dark, light - warm / cool + portrait colour) non-paint, opaque or transparent paint.

Two brushes (if using paint), white toned or coloured paper (a little larger).

Begin:

Copy two different parts of the portrait from the MMM observation (head, eye, ears).

Plan the light source and paint unimportant areas before important parts.

Use thin paint (large brush) and only show what is necessary.

Use larger brush for larger areas and paint smaller parts later - thin paint before using thick paint.

Decide the dominant colours and under-paint accordingly.

Suggest texture by dry-brush or sgraffito techniques and under-paint beforehand.

Then:

Paint the background to establish brightness of the painting (light/dark).

Paint dark and light areas to show the shape of the portrait.

Use soft and hard edges for modelling the shape - work from most distant to closest areas.

Boundary between shapes isn't always sharp or precise.

Develop your experiment but do NOT overwork it.

Gradually modify tones and colours – using cool before warm to show depth.

Conclude:

Clean up.

UNIT 3: Experiment 6

Start based on a different MMM portrait observation you have made.

Materials:

Your choice of (dark, light - warm / cool + portrait colour) non-paint, opaque or transparent paint.

Two brushes (if using paint), white toned or coloured paper (a little larger).

Begin:

Copy two different parts of the portrait from the MMM observation (head, eye, ears).

Plan the light source.

Paint unimportant areas before important parts.

Use thin paint (large brush) and only show what is necessary.

Use larger brush for larger areas and paint smaller parts later.

Use thin paint before using thick paint.

Decide the dominant colours and under-paint accordingly.

Suggest texture by dry-brush or sgraffito techniques and under-paint beforehand.

Then:

Note direction of the light and keep it consistent through the experiment.

Paint the background to establish brightness of the painting (light/dark).

Paint dark and light areas to show the shape of the portrait.

Use soft and hard edges for modelling the shape.

Work from most distant to closest areas.

Boundary between shapes isn't always sharp or precise.

Develop your experiment but do NOT overwork it.

Gradually modify tones and colours – using cool before warm to show depth.

Conclude:

Clean up.

Further thoughts:

Paint portraits doing different things.

Paint background to suggest shape of portrait.

Paint a portrait with as few brushstrokes as possible.

Use a spotlight to experiment with different sources and directions of lighting.

Focus on soft and hard edges for modelling the shape of a portrait.

DEVELOPMENT: Extensions

In the Development extension activities:

Draw on what you have learnt.

You can link what you have learned to your own goals.

DEVELOPMENT: Extension 1

Start with an MMM observation.

Materials:

Use the SAME materials as used in a previous experiment from Unit One.

Use the SAME MMM image as used in a previous experiment Unit One.

Begin:

BUT repeat only one of the experiments.

DEVELOPMENT: Extension 2

Start based on an MMM observation you have made.

Materials:

Use the SAME materials as used in a previous experiment from Unit Two.

Use the SAME MMM image as used in a previous experiment Unit Two.

Begin:

BUT repeat only one of the experiments.

DEVELOPMENT: Extension 3

Start based memory of an MMM observation you have made.

Materials:

Use the SAME materials as used in a previous experiment from Unit Three.

Use the SAMEMMM image as used in a previous experiment Unit Three.

Begin:

BUT repeat only one of the experiments.

3. MORE OBSERVED PORTRAITS.

FIRST Experience Unit:

UNIT 1: Experiment 1

Start with a MMM portrait observation you have made.

Materials:

Your choice of (dark, light - warm / cool / portrait colour) non-paint, opaque or transparent paint.

Two brushes (if using paint), white toned or coloured paper (a little larger).

Begin:

Copy two different parts of the portrait from the MMM observation (head, eye, ears).

Plan the light source.

Paint unimportant areas before important parts.

Decide the dominant colours plan under-painting.

Use thin paint (larger brush) before using thick paint.

Only show what is necessary.

Paint smaller parts later.

Suggest texture by dry-brush or sgraffito techniques and under-paint beforehand.

Then:

Keep direction of light consistent through the experiment.

Paint the background to establish brightness of the painting (light/dark).

Paint dark and light areas to show the shape of the portrait.

Boundary between shapes isn't always sharp or precise.

Use soft and hard edges for modelling the shape.

Work from most distant to closest areas.

Develop your experiment but do NOT overwork it.

Gradually modify tones and colours – using cool before warm to show depth.

Conclude:

Clean up.

UNIT 1: Experiment 2

Start with a MMM portrait observation you have made.

Materials:

Your choice of (dark, light - warm / cool / portrait colour) non-paint, opaque or transparent paint.

Two brushes (if using paint), white toned or coloured paper (a little larger).

Begin:

Copy two different parts of the portrait from the MMM observation (head, eye, ears).

Plan the light source.

Paint unimportant areas before important parts.

Decide the dominant colours plan under-painting.

Use thin paint (larger brush) before using thick paint.

Only show what is necessary.

Paint smaller parts later.

Suggest texture by dry-brush or sgraffito techniques and under-paint beforehand.

Then:

Keep direction of light consistent through the experiment.

Paint the background to establish brightness of the painting (light/dark).

Paint dark and light areas to show the shape of the portrait.

Boundary between shapes isn't always sharp or precise.

Use soft and hard edges for modelling the shape.

Work from most distant to closest areas.

Develop your experiment but do NOT overwork it.

Gradually modify tones and colours – using cool before warm to show depth.

Conclude:

Clean up.

UNIT 1: Experiment 3

Start with a MMM portrait observation you have made.

Materials:

Your choice of (dark, light - warm / cool + portrait colour) non-paint, opaque or transparent paint.

Two brushes (if using paint), white toned or coloured paper (a little larger).

Begin:

Copy two different parts of the portrait from the MMM observation (head, eye, ears).

Plan light source - paint unimportant areas before important with thin (larger brush) before thick.

Decide the dominant colours.

Under-paint to only show what is necessary - start with larger areas and paint smaller parts later.

Suggest texture by dry-brush or sgraffito techniques and under-paint beforehand.

Then:

Keep direction of light consistent through the experiment.

Paint the background to establish brightness of the painting (light/dark).

Paint dark and light areas to show the shape of the portrait.

Boundary between shapes isn't always sharp or precise - use soft and hard edges for modelling.

Work from most distant to closest areas.

Develop your experiment but do NOT overwork it.

Gradually modify tones and colours – using cool before warm to show depth.

Conclude:

Clean up.

UNIT 1: Experiment 4

Start with a MMM portrait observation you have made.

Materials:

Your choice of (dark, light - warm / cool + portrait colour) non-paint, opaque or transparent paint.

Two brushes (if using paint), white toned or coloured paper (a little larger).

Begin:

Copy two different parts of the portrait from the MMM observation (head, eye, ears).

Plan the light source.

Paint unimportant areas before important parts with thin (larger brush) before thick paint.

Decide the dominant colours.

Plan the under-painting to only show what is necessary.

Start with larger areas and paint smaller parts later.

Suggest texture by dry-brush or sgraffito techniques and under-paint beforehand.

Then:

Keep direction of light consistent through the experiment.

Paint the background to establish brightness of the portrait (light/dark).

Work from most distant to closest areas.

Paint dark and light areas to show the shape of the portrait.

Boundary between shapes isn't always sharp or precise.

Use soft and hard edges for modelling the shape.

Develop your experiment but do NOT overwork it.

Gradually modify tones and colours – using cool before warm to show depth.

Conclude:

Clean up.

UNIT 1: Experiment 5

Start with a MMM portrait observation you have made.

Materials:

Your choice of (dark, light - warm / cool + portrait colour) non-paint, opaque or transparent paint.

Two brushes (if using paint), white toned or coloured paper (a little larger).

Begin:

Copy two different parts of the portrait from the MMM observation (head, eye, ears).

Plan the light source and keep direction of light consistent through the experiment.

Paint unimportant areas before important parts with thin (larger brush) before thick paint.

Start with larger areas and paint smaller parts later.

Decide the dominant colours.

Plan the under-painting to only show what is necessary.

Suggest texture by dry-brush or sgraffito techniques and under-paint beforehand.

Then:

Paint the background to establish brightness of the portrait (light/dark).

Work from most distant to closest areas.

Paint dark and light areas to show shape of the portrait - use soft and hard edges for modelling.

Develop your experiment but do NOT overwork it.

Gradually modify tones and colours – using cool before warm to show depth.

Conclude:

Clean up.

UNIT 1: Experiment 6

Start with a MMM portrait observation you have made.

Materials:

Your choice of (dark, light - warm / cool + portrait colour) non-paint, opaque or transparent paint.

Two brushes (if using paint), white toned or coloured paper (a little larger).

Begin:

Copy three different parts of the portrait from the MMM observation (head, eye, ears).

Plan the light source and keep direction of light consistent through the experiment.

Paint unimportant areas before important parts with thin (larger brush) before thick paint.

Start with larger areas and paint smaller parts later.

Decide the dominant colours.

Plan the under-painting to only show what is necessary.

Suggest texture by dry-brush or sgraffito techniques and under-paint beforehand.

Then:

Paint the background to establish brightness of the portrait (light/dark).

Work from most distant to closest areas.

Paint dark and light areas to show the shape of the portrait.

Use soft and hard edges for modelling the shape.

Develop your experiment but do NOT overwork it.

Gradually modify tones and colours – using cool before warm to show depth.

Conclude:

Clean up.

Further thoughts:

Use different combinations of parts of the portrait from the MMM observation (head, eye, ears).

Try another portrait.

SECOND Experience Unit:

UNIT 2: Experiment 1

Start with a MMM portrait observation you have made.

Materials:

Your choice of (dark, light - warm / cool + portrait colour) non-paint, opaque or transparent paint.

Three brushes (if using paint), white toned or coloured paper (a little larger).

Begin:

Copy three parts of the portrait from a MMM observation (eyes, nose, mouth) not whole portrait.

Plan the light source and keep direction of light consistent through the experiment.

Paint unimportant areas before important parts with thin (larger brush) before thick paint.

Start with larger areas and paint smaller parts later.

Decide the dominant colours and plan the under-painting to only show what is necessary.

Suggest texture by dry-brush or sgraffito techniques and under-paint beforehand.

Then:

Paint the background to establish brightness of the portrait (light/dark).

Work from most distant to closest areas.

Paint dark and light areas to show the shape of the portrait.

Use soft and hard edges for modelling the shape.

Develop your experiment but do NOT overwork it.

Gradually modify tones and colours – using cool before warm to show depth.

Conclude:

Clean up.

UNIT 2: Experiment 2

Start with a MMM portrait observation you have made.

Materials:

Your choice of (dark, light - warm / cool + portrait colour) non-paint, opaque or transparent paint.

Three brushes (if using paint), white toned or coloured paper (a little larger).

Begin:

Copy three parts of the portrait from a MMM observation (eyes, nose, mouth) not whole portrait.

Plan the light source and keep direction of light consistent through the experiment.

Paint unimportant areas before important parts with thin (larger brush) before thick paint.

Start with larger areas and paint smaller parts later.

Decide the dominant colours and plan the under-painting to only show what is necessary.

Suggest texture by dry-brush or sgraffito techniques and under-paint beforehand.

Then:

Paint the background to establish brightness of the portrait (light/dark).

Work from most distant to closest areas.

Paint dark and light areas to show the shape of the portrait.

Use soft and hard edges for modelling the shape.

Develop your experiment but do NOT overwork it.

Gradually modify tones and colours – using cool before warm to show depth.

Conclude:

Clean up.

UNIT 2: Experiment 3

Start with a MMM portrait observation you have made.

Materials:

Your choice of (dark, light - warm / cool + portrait colour) non-paint, opaque or transparent paint.

Three brushes (if using paint), white toned or coloured paper (a little larger).

Begin:

Copy three parts of the portrait from a MMM observation (eyes, nose, mouth) not whole portrait.

Plan the light source and keep direction of light consistent through the experiment.

Paint unimportant areas before important parts with thin (larger brush) before thick paint.

Start with larger areas and paint smaller parts later.

Decide the dominant colours and plan the under-painting to only show what is necessary.

Suggest texture by dry-brush or sgraffito techniques and under-paint beforehand.

Then:

Paint the background to establish brightness of the portrait (light/dark).

Work from most distant to closest areas.

Paint dark and light areas to show the shape of the portrait.

Use soft and hard edges for modelling the shape.

Develop your experiment but do NOT overwork it.

Gradually modify tones and colours – using cool before warm to show depth.

Conclude:

Clean up.

UNIT 2: Experiment 4

Start with a MMM portrait observation you have made.

Materials:

Your choice of (dark, light - warm / cool + portrait colour) non-paint, opaque or transparent paint.

Three brushes (if using paint), white toned or coloured paper (a little larger).

Begin:

Copy the portrait from a MMM observation (whole portrait).

Plan the light source and keep direction of light consistent through the experiment.

Paint unimportant areas before important parts with thin (larger brush) before thick paint.

Start with larger areas and paint smaller parts later.

Decide the dominant colours and plan the under-painting to only show what is necessary.

Suggest texture by dry-brush or sgraffito techniques and under-paint beforehand.

Then:

Paint the background to establish brightness of the portrait (light/dark).

Work from most distant to closest areas.

Paint dark and light areas to show the shape of the portrait.

Use soft and hard edges for modelling the shape.

Develop your experiment but do NOT overwork it.

Gradually modify tones and colours – using cool before warm to show depth.

Conclude:

Clean up.

UNIT 2: Experiment 5

Start with a MMM portrait observation you have made.

Materials:

Your choice of (dark, light - warm / cool + portrait colour) non-paint, opaque or transparent paint.

Three brushes (if using paint), white toned or coloured paper (a little larger).

Begin:

Copy the portrait from the MMM observation.

Plan the light source and keep direction of light consistent through the experiment.

Paint unimportant areas before important parts with thin before thick paint.

Large brushes before small brushes.

Start with larger areas and paint smaller parts later.

Decide the dominant colours and plan the under-painting to only show what is necessary.

Suggest texture by dry-brush or sgraffito techniques and under-paint beforehand.

Then:

Paint the background to establish brightness of the portrait (light/dark).

Work from most distant to closest areas.

Paint dark and light areas to show the shape of the portrait.

Use soft and hard edges for modelling the shape.

Develop your experiment but do NOT overwork it.

Gradually modify tones and colours – using cool before warm to show depth.

Conclude:

Clean up.

UNIT 2: Experiment 6

Start with a MMM portrait observation you have made.

Materials:

Your choice of (dark, light - warm / cool + portrait colour) non-paint, opaque or transparent paint.

Three brushes (if using paint), white toned or coloured paper (a little larger).

Begin:

Copy the portrait from the MMM observation.

Plan the light source and keep direction of light consistent through the experiment.

Paint unimportant areas before important parts with thin before thick paint.

Large brushes before small brushes.

Start with larger areas and paint smaller parts later.

Decide the dominant colours and plan the under-painting to only show what is necessary.

Suggest texture by dry-brush or sgraffito techniques and under-paint beforehand.

Then:

Paint the background to establish brightness of the portrait (light/dark).

Work from most distant to closest areas.

Paint dark and light areas to show the shape of the portrait.

Use soft and hard edges for modelling the shape.

Develop your experiment but do NOT overwork it.

Gradually modify tones and colours – using cool before warm to show depth.

Conclude:

Clean up.

Further thoughts:

Experiment with different viewpoints of the portrait (above, front, side).

Try different portraits from time to time.

They are a similar combination of different elements.

Look for characteristic arrangements for that portrait.

Correct colour can come later.

THIRD Experience Unit:

UNIT 3: Experiment 1

Start with a MMM portrait observation you have made.

Materials:

Your choice of (dark, light - warm / cool + portrait colour) non-paint, opaque or transparent paint.

Three brushes (if using paint), white toned or coloured paper (a little larger).

Begin:

Copy the portrait from the MMM observation.

Plan the light source and keep direction of light consistent through the experiment.

Paint unimportant areas before important parts with thin before thick paint.

Large brushes before small brushes.

Start with larger areas and paint smaller parts later.

Decide the dominant colours and plan the under-painting to only show what is necessary.

Suggest texture by dry-brush or sgraffito techniques and under-paint beforehand.

Then:

Paint the background to establish brightness of the portrait (light/dark).

Work from most distant to closest areas.

Paint dark and light areas to show the shape of the portrait.

Use soft and hard edges for modelling the shape.

Develop your experiment but do NOT overwork it.

Gradually modify tones and colours – using cool before warm to show depth.

Conclude:

Clean up.

UNIT 3: Experiment 2

Start with a different MMM portrait observation you have made.

Materials:

Your choice of (dark, light - warm / cool + portrait colour) non-paint, opaque or transparent paint.

Three brushes (if using paint), white toned or coloured paper (a little larger).

Begin:

Copy the portrait from the MMM observation.

Plan the light source and keep direction of light consistent through the experiment.

Paint unimportant areas before important parts with thin before thick paint.

Large brushes before small brushes.

Start with larger areas and paint smaller parts later.

Decide the dominant colours and plan the under-painting to only show what is necessary.

Suggest texture by dry-brush or sgraffito techniques and under-paint beforehand.

Then:

Paint the background to establish brightness of the portrait (light/dark).

Work from most distant to closest areas.

Paint dark and light areas to show the shape of the portrait.

Use soft and hard edges for modelling the shape.

Develop your experiment but do NOT overwork it.

Gradually modify tones and colours – using cool before warm to show depth.

Conclude:

Clean up.

UNIT 3: Experiment 3

Start with another MMM portrait observation you have made.

Materials:

Your choice of (dark, light - warm / cool + portrait colour) non-paint, opaque or transparent paint.

Three brushes (if using paint), white toned or coloured paper (a little larger).

Begin:

Copy the portrait from the MMM observation.

Plan the light source and keep direction of light consistent through the experiment.

Paint unimportant areas before important parts with thin before thick paint.

Large brushes before small brushes.

Start with larger areas and paint smaller parts later.

Decide the dominant colours and plan the under-painting to only show what is necessary.

Suggest texture by dry-brush or sgraffito techniques and under-paint beforehand.

Then:

Paint the background to establish brightness of the portrait (light/dark).

Work from most distant to closest areas.

Paint dark and light areas to show the shape of the portrait.

Use soft and hard edges for modelling the shape.

Develop your experiment but do NOT overwork it.

Gradually modify tones and colours – using cool before warm to show depth.

Conclude:

Clean up.

UNIT 3: Experiment 4

Start with two MMM portrait observations you have made.

Materials:

Your choice of (dark, light - warm / cool + portrait colour) non-paint, opaque or transparent paint.

Three brushes (if using paint), white toned or coloured paper (a little larger).

Begin:

Combine the portraits from the MMM observation in your experiment.

Plan the light source and keep direction of light consistent through the experiment.

Paint unimportant areas before important parts with thin before thick paint.

Large brushes before small brushes.

Start with larger areas and paint smaller parts later.

Decide the dominant colours and plan the under-painting to only show what is necessary.

Suggest texture by dry-brush or sgraffito techniques and under-paint beforehand.

Then:

Paint the background to establish brightness of the portrait (light/dark).

Work from most distant to closest areas.

Paint dark and light areas to show the shape of the portrait.

Use soft and hard edges for modelling the shape.

Develop your experiment but do NOT overwork it.

Gradually modify tones and colours – using cool before warm to show depth.

Conclude:

Clean up.

UNIT 3: Experiment 5

Start with two MMM portrait observations you have made.

Materials:

Your choice of (dark, light - warm / cool + portrait colour) non-paint, opaque or transparent paint.

Three brushes (if using paint), white toned or coloured paper (a little larger).

Begin:

Combine the portraits from the MMM observation in your experiment.

Plan the light source and keep direction of light consistent through the experiment.

Paint unimportant areas before important parts with thin before thick paint.

Large brushes before small brushes.

Start with larger areas and paint smaller parts later.

Decide the dominant colours and plan the under-painting to only show what is necessary.

Suggest texture by dry-brush or sgraffito techniques and under-paint beforehand.

Then:

Paint the background to establish brightness of the portrait (light/dark).

Work from most distant to closest areas.

Paint dark and light areas to show the shape of the portrait.

Use soft and hard edges for modelling the shape.

Develop your experiment but do NOT overwork it.

Gradually modify tones and colours – using cool before warm to show depth.

Conclude:

Clean up.

UNIT3: Experiment 6

Start with several MMM portrait observations you have made.

Materials:

Your choice of (dark, light - warm / cool + portrait colour) non-paint, opaque or transparent paint.

Three brushes (if using paint), white toned or coloured paper (a little larger).

Begin:

Combine the portraits from the MMM observation as a group in your experiment.

Plan the light source and keep direction of light consistent through the experiment.

Paint unimportant areas before important parts with thin before thick paint.

Large brushes before small brushes.

Start with larger areas and paint smaller parts later.

Decide the dominant colours and plan the under-painting to only show what is necessary.

Suggest texture by dry-brush or sgraffito techniques and under-paint beforehand.

Then:

Paint the background to establish brightness of the portrait (light/dark).

Work from most distant to closest areas.

Paint dark and light areas to show the shape of the portrait.

Use soft and hard edges for modelling the shape.

Develop your experiment but do NOT overwork it.

Gradually modify tones and colours – using cool before warm to show depth.

Conclude:

Clean up.

Further thoughts:
Experiment with different groups of the portrait.
Also experiment with different viewpoints (top, side, rear, front) of the portrait.
Try different portraits from time to time.
They are a similar combination of different elements.
Look for characteristic arrangements for that portrait.
Correct colour can come later.

Make a study box.
Cut down a box so it is like a small room with a floor and two or even three sides.
Toy portraits can be placed in the study box.
The floor and walls can be painted differently from time to time.

DEVELOPMENT: Extensions

In the Development extension activities:

Draw on what you have learnt.

You can link what you have learned to your own goals.

DEVELOPMENT: Extension 1

Start with an MMM observation.

Materials:

Use the SAME materials as used in a previous experiment from Unit One.

Use the SAME MMM image as used in a previous experiment Unit One.

Begin:

BUT repeat only one of the experiments.

DEVELOPMENT: Extension 2

Start based on an MMM observation you have made.

Materials:

Use the SAME materials as used in a previous experiment from Unit Two.

Use the SAME MMM image as used in a previous experiment Unit Two.

Begin:

BUT repeat only one of the experiments.

DEVELOPMENT: Extension 3

Start based memory of an MMM observation you have made.

Materials:

Use the SAME materials as used in a previous experiment from Unit Three.

Use the SAME MMM image as used in a previous experiment Unit Three.

Begin:

BUT repeat only one of the experiments.

CONGRATULATIONS.

You have taken the OBSERVATION pathway.
This continues from the previous pattern of experiments.
The focus is on observation as a basis for a continuing search for reality.
This could be the final step to being the artist you want to be.

But perhaps you want to try them all?
Then follow the sequence of MMM experiments as outlined.
There is a logical progression.

The third pathway is linked to your IMAGINATION.
This focus is more personal.
But again there is a foundation from the MMM experiments.

Your MMM experiments are like the athletes training program.

But the training never stops.
Olympic athletes want to remain at the highest level so must keep training.
Your MMM experiments become a normal routine to do the same.

Make notes, do sketches and record what you can see.
This is material you can draw on when continuing your MMM experiments.
Make a habit to carry a small sketchpad or scraps of paper and a pen or pencil.

Perhaps start each day with a short period of experiments.
Then move to your main artistic tasks.

You'll need to construct YOUR OWN MMM experimental programs.
By now this should not be difficult.

4. IMAGINARY PORTRAITS.

Limited materials will encourage more thoughtful responses.
Creativity, an ability to do most with least, is developed.
In art as in science the task of combining many variables is highly skilled.
Repeat something rather than use too great a variety of materials.

The artist, during the act of creating a work is expressing something.
Expression is a unique personal action.

For example three artists attempt to paint the same subject, exactly as seen.
They will finish with three different works.
The differences can be attributed to the various artists' expression.
Their works are symbols for this expression.

Expression is related to emotion.
Although the individual may not be conscious of what that emotion is.
The presence of emotion creates a tension (a feeling).
This tension is not necessarily that emotion, but an awareness of an emotional state.

Expression is bringing into perceptual shape symbols for that awareness.
It is thus related to that the underlying emotional state.

The expressive act is not necessarily related to any particular audience.
There is a difference between arousing emotion in an audience, which is intended.
This is manipulative and a shape of communication.

A similar arousal can be the result of expression.
Such expression denotes and belongs to an individual.
It is actually a characteristic of individuals.

It is not a shape of communication although observers are often mistaken in this regard.

There is a difference between emotion and exhibiting symptoms of emotion.
The former is necessary for artistic activity and is a personal reaction to a stimulus.
Symptoms of emotion are what an observer sees.
They may be manipulation of the appropriate symbols without any emotion at all (like an actor).

The relationship between an artist and the work is thus a personal one.
It is linked to the inner state of the artist prior to, and during, the process of creating.
That may ultimately be a work of art.

It doesn't really matter what you do at the start.
The most important thing is to actually do something.
Let's see what happens here when I do this?

Random starts do not necessarily have to be the case.
You can plan your starts.
But take your time.
Don't rush enjoy the experience and see what you can find out.

Once you begin, you can alter or change what you have done.
It's better to do something and be wrong, than do nothing.
Mistakes can be corrected, and you learn what not to do at the same time.
Any experiment does not even have to be finished!

In the process you'll discover whatever you find out.
More importantly the discoveries are yours.
They are part of your actual experience rather than just part of following instructions.

Your knowledge grows from your own experiences.
This is what real learning is about.
Your experience and confidence grows for the more you do the better you get!

You are the judge of quality, which is a variable that changes over time.
You probably have old works that you thought were excellent at the time they were done.
What are they like now?

Continue with the subject matter you want to paint really well.
That way you are continuing down the correct path (for you).
Your focus is always on portraits.

But now you are imagining your chosen painting focus.
This means you are NOT limited to things you can actually look at.

You can make notes, do sketches and record what you can see.
This is material you can draw on when continuing your MMM experiments.
Make a habit of carrying a small sketchpad or even scraps of paper and a pen or pencil.

Observation helps you understand what you look at or whatever you like.
Over time you will develop the individual paining skills needed.
You will also know how to paint your subject your way.
That means you can take liberties in regard to what you see.

Eventually you can focus on another subject.
If it is related to your original theme you will learn much quicker.
From one breed of dog to another is an example.
Then from one kind of portrait to another.
That means you can take liberties in regard to what you see.

You'll note the similarities and also the differences.

Totally imaginary landscapes are an extension of this process.

Follow this pattern for long enough, and you'll be able to paint anything!

People who do things well also do them faster than those who don't.

That applies to painting just as much as anything else.

It's one of the indicators of skill.

By now you should have noticed that repetition helps skill development.

Several small paintings are better for learning than a larger one (just take time).

That's how you can apply what you have learnt.

Skill in art, sport or even medicine is basically the same phenomenon.

It's practiced behaviour in action.

Most artists don't do anywhere near enough paintings to develop any real skill.

Increase productivity, work on a number of experiments at the same time

For you reduce wasted time.

Once you run into a dead-end with a painting move to another for a fresh start.

When the initial painting is returned to, there will be a different attitude, or set it aside again.

Working on a number of experiments at the same time also saves materials.

A particular colour can be applied to the work for which it was intended.

BUT there are bound to be other works where that same colour will be appropriate.

When you buy paint, buy in quantity, but only use as needed.

Avoid major works.

They take time (even years), are usually done slowly and are often large and complex.

You'll tend to labour over them as you seek to do your best.

You might occasionally do a slightly larger experiment.

Focus on learning what you can.

Action with materials = technique.

Practiced techniques = skill.

Habitual technique + skill = style.

NOW START: IMAGINARY PORTRAITS

FIRST Experience Unit:

UNIT 1: Experiment 1

Imagine a distorted MMM image to start.

Materials:

Dark/light, warm/cool, dominant colour, non-paint, opaque or transparent.

Three brushes (if using paint), white toned or coloured paper (a little larger).

Preparation:

Distort the portrait from the MMM image in your experiment.

Add another image (not portrait) into the experiment.

Decide the dominant colour.

Consider the tonal arrangement.

Think about the spaces

Begin:

Large brushes before small brushes.

Start with larger areas and paint smaller parts later – basic construction.

Paint unimportant areas before important parts but only what is essential.

Thin before thick paint.

Then:

Paint the background to establish brightness of the portrait (light/dark).

Under-paint with the dominant colour.

Paint dark and light areas to show the shape of the portrait.

Now:

Gradually modify tones and colours – using cool before warm to show depth.

Use tone to show depth (perspective) – light to dark.

Lightest tone most distant.

Continue:

Use soft and hard edges for modelling the shape.

Suggest texture by dry-brush or sgraffito and under-paint beforehand.

Develop your experiment but do NOT overwork it.

Conclude: Clean up.

UNIT 1: Experiment 2

Imagine a distorted MMM image to start.

Materials:

Choice of (dark, light - warm / cool + dominant colour) non-paint, opaque or transparent paint.

Three brushes (if using paint), white toned or coloured paper (a little larger).

Preparation:

Distort the portrait from the MMM image in your experiment.

Add another image (not portrait) into the experiment.

Decide the dominant colour.

Consider the tonal arrangement.

Think about the spaces

Begin:

Start with larger areas and paint smaller parts later – basic construction.

Paint unimportant areas before important parts.

But only what is essential.

Then:

Paint the background to establish brightness of the portrait (light/dark).

Under-paint with the dominant colour.

Paint dark and light areas to show the shape of the portrait.

Thin before thick paint.

Cool colour before warm.

Now:

Gradually modify tones and colours – using cool before warm to show depth.

Use tone to show depth (perspective) – darkest tone most distant.

Continue:

Use soft and hard edges for modelling the shape.

Suggest texture by dry-brush or sgraffito techniques and under-paint beforehand.

Develop your experiment but do NOT overwork it.

Conclude:

Clean up.

UNIT 1: Experiment 3

Imagine a distorted MMM image to start.

Materials:

Choice of (dark, light - warm / cool + dominant colour) non-paint, opaque or transparent paint.

Three brushes (if using paint), white toned or coloured paper (a little larger).

Preparation:

Distort the portrait from the MMM image in your experiment.

Add another image (not portrait) into the experiment.

Decide the dominant colour.

Consider the tonal arrangement.

Think about the spaces

Begin:

Start with larger areas and paint smaller parts later – basic construction.

Paint unimportant areas before important parts.

But only what is essential.

Then:

Paint the background to establish brightness of the portrait (light/dark).

Under-paint with the dominant colour.

Paint dark and light areas to show the shape of the portrait.

Thin before thick paint.

Cool colour before warm.

Now:

Gradually modify tones and colours – using cool before warm to show depth.

Use tone to show depth (perspective) – darkest tone most distant.

Continue:

Use soft and hard edges for modelling the shape.

Suggest texture by dry-brush or sgraffito techniques and under-paint beforehand.

Develop your experiment but do NOT overwork it.

Conclude:

Clean up.

UNIT 1: Experiment 4

Imagine a distorted MMM image to start.

Materials:

Choice of (dark, light - warm / cool + dominant colour) non-paint, opaque or transparent paint.

Three brushes (if using paint), white toned or coloured paper (a little larger).

Preparation:

Distort the portrait from the MMM image in your experiment.

Add two other images (not portrait) into the experiment.

Decide the dominant colour.

Consider the tonal arrangement.

Think about the spaces

Begin:

Start with larger areas and paint smaller parts later – basic construction.

Paint unimportant areas before important parts.

But only what is essential.

Then:

Paint the background to establish brightness of the portrait (light/dark).

Under-paint with the dominant colour.

Paint dark and light areas to show the shape of the portrait.

Thin before thick paint.

Cool colour before warm.

Now:

Gradually modify tones and colours – using cool before warm to show depth.

Use tone to show depth (perspective) – darkest tone most distant.

Continue:

Use soft and hard edges for modelling the shape.

Suggest texture by dry-brush or sgraffito techniques and under-paint beforehand.

Develop your experiment but do NOT overwork it.

Conclude:

Clean up.

UNIT 1: Experiment 5

Imagine a distorted MMM image to start.

Materials:

Choice of (dark, light - warm / cool + dominant colour) non-paint, opaque or transparent paint.

Three brushes (if using paint), white toned or coloured paper (a little larger).

Preparation:

Distort the portrait from the MMM image in your experiment.

Add two other images (not portrait) into the experiment.

Decide the dominant colour.

Consider the tonal arrangement.

Think about the spaces

Begin:

Start with larger areas and paint smaller parts later – basic construction.

Paint unimportant areas before important parts.

But only what is essential.

Then:

Paint the background to establish brightness of the portrait (light/dark).

Under-paint with the dominant colour.

Paint dark and light areas to show the shape of the portrait.

Thin before thick paint.

Cool colour before warm.

Now:

Gradually modify tones and colours – using cool before warm to show depth.

Use tone to show depth (perspective) – darkest tone most distant.

Continue:

Use soft and hard edges for modelling the shape.

Suggest texture by dry-brush or sgraffito techniques and under-paint beforehand.

Develop your experiment but do NOT overwork it.

Conclude:

Clean up.

UNIT 1: Experiment 6

Imagine a distorted MMM image to start.

Materials:

Choice of (dark, light - warm / cool + dominant colour) non-paint, opaque or transparent paint.

Three brushes (if using paint), white toned or coloured paper (a little larger).

Preparation:

Distort the portrait from the MMM image in your experiment.

Add two other images (not portrait) into the experiment.

Decide the dominant colour.

Consider the tonal arrangement.

Think about the spaces

Begin:

Start with larger areas and paint smaller parts later – basic construction.

Paint unimportant areas before important parts.

But only what is essential.

Then:

Focus experiment on colour.

Paint the background to establish brightness of the portrait (light/dark).

Under-paint with the dominant colour.

Paint dark and light areas to show the shape of the portrait.

Thin before thick paint.

Cool colour before warm.

Now:

Gradually modify tones and colours – using cool before warm to show depth.

Use tone to show depth (perspective) – darkest tone most distant.

Continue:

Use soft and hard edges for modelling the shape.

Suggest texture by dry-brush or sgraffito techniques and under-paint beforehand.

Develop your experiment but do NOT overwork it.

Conclude:

Clean up.

Further thoughts:

Experiment with the focus on different elements (colour, tone, shape, line, etc.).

Also experiment with different principles (harmony, contrast, etc.).

Also vary the viewpoint of your imaginary portrait.

SECOND Experience Unit:

UNIT 2: Experiment 1

Imagine a semi-abstract MMM image to start.

Consider the visual element: Space

The factor that indicates emptiness or a break.

Space relates to the lack of obvious other element (particularly mass and line).

However space usually relates to being inside, outside, under or over.

Space may be open (incomplete) or closed (has a boundary).

Space also may be actual or implied.

It is sometimes termed environment.

Materials:

Choice of (dark, light - warm / cool + dominant colour) non-paint, opaque or transparent paint.

Three brushes (if using paint), white toned or coloured paper (a little larger).

Preparation:

Distort the portrait from the MMM image in your experiment.

Add two or more other images (not portrait) into the experiment.

Decide the dominant colour.

Consider the tonal arrangement.

Think about the spaces

Begin:

Start with larger areas and paint smaller parts later – basic construction.

Paint unimportant areas before important parts.

But only what is essential.

Then:

Focus experiment on colour.

Paint the background to establish brightness of the portrait (light/dark).

Under-paint with the dominant colour.

Paint dark and light areas to show the shape of the portrait.

Thin before thick paint.

Cool colour before warm.

Now:

Gradually modify tones and colours – using cool before warm to show depth.

Use tone to show depth (perspective) – lightest tone most distant.

Continue:

Use soft and hard edges for modelling the shape.

Suggest texture by dry-brush or sgraffito techniques and under-paint beforehand.

Develop your experiment but do NOT overwork it.

Conclude:

Clean up.

UNIT 2: Experiment 2

Imagine a semi-abstract MMM image to start.

Consider the visual element: Space

The factor that indicates emptiness or a break.

Space relates to the lack of obvious other element (particularly mass and line).

However space usually relates to being inside, outside, under or over.

Space may be open (incomplete) or closed (has a boundary).

Space also may be actual or implied.

Materials:

Choice of (dark, light - warm / cool + dominant colour) non-paint, opaque or transparent paint.

Three brushes (if using paint), white toned or coloured paper (a little larger).

Preparation:

Distort the portrait from the MMM image in your experiment.

Add two or more other images (not portrait) into the experiment.

Decide the dominant colour.

Consider the tonal arrangement.

Think about the spaces

Begin:

Start with larger areas and paint smaller parts later – basic construction.

Paint unimportant areas before important parts.

But only what is essential.

Then:

Focus experiment on colour.

Paint the background to establish brightness of the portrait (light/dark).

Under-paint with the dominant colour.

Paint dark and light areas to show the shape of the portrait.

Thin before thick paint.

Cool colour before warm.

Now:

Gradually modify tones and colours – using cool before warm to show depth.

Use tone to show depth (perspective) – darkest tone most distant.

Continue:

Use soft and hard edges for modelling the shape.

Suggest texture by dry-brush or sgraffito techniques and under-paint beforehand.

Develop your experiment but do NOT overwork it.

Conclude:

Clean up.

UNIT 2: Experiment 3

Imagine a semi-abstract MMM image to start.

Consider the visual element: Space

The factor that indicates emptiness or a break.

However space usually relates to being inside, outside, under or over.

Space may be open (incomplete) or closed (has a boundary).

Space also may be actual or implied.

Materials:

Choice of (dark, light - warm / cool + dominant colour) non-paint, opaque or transparent paint.

Three brushes (if using paint), white toned or coloured paper (a little larger).

Preparation:

Distort the portrait from the MMM image in your experiment.

Add two or more other distorted images (not portrait) into the experiment.

Decide the dominant colour.

Consider the tonal arrangement.

Think about the spaces

Begin:

Start with larger areas and paint smaller parts later – basic construction.

Paint unimportant areas before important parts.

But only what is essential.

Then:

Focus experiment on colour.

Paint the background to establish brightness of the portrait (light/dark).

Under-paint with the dominant colour.

Paint dark and light areas to show the shape of the portrait.

Thin before thick paint.

Cool colour before warm.

Now:

Gradually modify tones and colours – using cool before warm to show depth.

Use tone to show depth (perspective) – lightest and darkest tone closest with grey most distant.

Continue:

Use soft and hard edges for modelling the shape.

Suggest texture by dry-brush or sgraffito techniques and under-paint beforehand.

Develop your experiment but do NOT overwork it.

Conclude:

Clean up.

UNIT 2: Experiment 4

Imagine a semi-abstract MMM image to start.

Consider the visual element: Space

Space usually relates to being inside, outside, under or over.

Space may be open (incomplete) or closed (has a boundary).

Space also may be actual or implied.

Materials:

Choice of (dark, light - warm / cool + dominant colour) non-paint, opaque or transparent paint.

Three brushes (if using paint), white toned or coloured paper (a little larger).

Preparation:

Distort the portrait from the MMM image in your experiment.

Add two or more other distorted images (not portrait) into the experiment.

Decide the dominant colour.

Consider the tonal arrangement.

Think about the spaces

Begin:

Start with larger areas and paint smaller parts later – basic construction.

Paint unimportant areas before important parts.

But only what is essential.

Then:

Focus experiment on colour.

Paint the background to establish brightness of the portrait (light/dark).

Under-paint with the dominant colour.

Paint dark and light areas to show the shape of the portrait.

Thin before thick paint.

Cool colour before warm.

Now:

Gradually modify tones and colours – using cool before warm to show depth.

Use tone show depth (perspective) – lightest and darkest closest, grey distant.

Continue:

Use soft and hard edges for modelling the shape.

Suggest texture dry-brush or sgraffito techniques and under-paint beforehand.

Develop your experiment but do NOT overwork it.

Conclude: Clean up.

UNIT 2: Experiment 5

Imagine a semi-abstract MMM image to start.

Consider the visual element: Space

Space may be open (incomplete) or closed (has a boundary).

Space also may be actual or implied.

Materials:

Choice of (dark, light - warm / cool + dominant colour) non-paint, opaque or transparent paint.

Three brushes (if using paint), white toned or coloured paper (a little larger).

Preparation:

Distort the portrait from the MMM image in your experiment.

Add two or more other overlapping and distorted images (not portrait)..

Decide the dominant colour.

Consider the tonal arrangement.

Think about the spaces

Begin:

Start with larger areas and paint smaller parts later – basic construction.

Paint unimportant areas before important parts.

But only what is essential.

Then:

Focus experiment on colour.

Paint the background to establish brightness of the portrait (light/dark).

Under-paint with the dominant colour.

Paint dark and light areas to show the shape of the portrait.

Thin before thick paint.

Cool colour before warm.

Now:

Gradually modify tones and colours – using cool before warm to show depth.

Tone to show depth (perspective) – lightest and darkest closest grey distant.

Continue:

Use soft and hard edges for modelling the shape.

Suggest texture by dry-brush or sgraffito techniques and under-paint beforehand.

Develop your experiment but do NOT overwork it.

Conclude: Clean up.

UNIT 2: Experiment 6

Imagine a semi-abstract MMM image to start.

Consider the visual element: Space

Space may be open (incomplete) or closed (has a boundary).

Materials:

Choice of (dark, light - warm / cool + dominant colour) non-paint, opaque or transparent paint.

Three brushes (if using paint), white toned or coloured paper (a little larger).

Preparation:

Distort the portrait from the MMM image in your experiment.

Add two or more overlapping and distorted images (not portrait) into the experiment.

Decide the dominant colour.

Consider the tonal arrangement.

Think about the spaces

Begin:

Start with larger areas and paint smaller parts later – basic construction.

Paint unimportant areas before important parts.

But only what is essential.

Then:

Focus experiment on colour.

Paint the background to establish brightness of the portrait (light/dark).

Under-paint with the dominant colour.

Paint dark and light areas to show the shape of the portrait.

Thin before thick paint.

Cool colour before warm.

Now:

Gradually modify tones and colours – using cool before warm to show depth.

Tone to show depth – lightest and darkest closest with grey distant.

Continue:

Refocus on the dominant colour and modify local colour accordingly.

Use soft and hard edges for modelling the shape.

Suggest texture by dry-brush or sgraffito and under-paint beforehand.

Develop your experiment but do NOT overwork it.

Conclude: Clean up.

Further thoughts:

Also experiment with different principles (harmony, contrast, etc.).

Also vary the viewpoint of your imaginary portrait.

Portraits have their own colour (local colour).

This could be any colour if you paint consistently.

THIRD Experience Unit:

UNIT 3: Experiment 1
Imagine two semi-abstracted MMM images to start.

Consider the visual element: Direction

The factor that indicates aim or course of movement.

The movement may be real or suggested.

Direction relates to a plane or axis, which may be horizontal, vertical or oblique.

There is a start and an end and can be seen in a serial order or sequence.

There is a link with rhythm and balance.

Materials:

Choice non-paint, opaque or transparent paint (dark, light, dominant, complementary) colours.

Three brushes (if using paint), white toned or coloured paper (a little larger).

Preparation:

Distort the portraits from the MMM images in your experiment.

Add two or more overlapping and distorted images (not portrait) into the experiment.

Decide the dominant colour.

Consider the tonal arrangement.

Think about the spaces

Begin:

Start with larger areas and paint smaller parts later – basic construction.

Paint unimportant areas before important parts.

But only what is essential.

Then:

Under-paint with the dominant colour.

Thin before thick paint.

Cool colour before warm.

Now:

Gradually modify tones and colours.

Use tone to show depth (perspective) – lightest and darkest tone closest with grey most distant.

Continue:

Refocus on the dominant colour and modify local colour accordingly.

Use the complementary (opposite) colours in short brushstrokes next to one another.

Use soft and hard edges for modelling.

Suggest texture by dry-brush or sgraffito techniques and under-paint beforehand.

Develop your experiment but do NOT overwork it.

Conclude:

Clean up.

UNIT 3: Experiment 2

Imagine two semi-abstracted MMM images to start.

Consider the visual element: Direction

The factor that indicates aim or course of movement.

The movement may be real or suggested.

Direction relates to a plane or axis, which may be horizontal, vertical or oblique.

There is a start and an end and can be seen in a serial order or sequence.

Materials:

Choice non-paint, opaque or transparent paint (dark, light, dominant, complementary) colours.

Three brushes (if using paint), white toned or coloured paper (a little larger).

Preparation:

Distort the portraits from the MMM images in your experiment.

Add two or more overlapping and distorted images (not portrait) into the experiment.

Decide the dominant colour.

Consider the tonal arrangement.

Think about the spaces

Begin:

Start with larger areas and paint smaller parts later – basic construction.

Paint unimportant areas before important parts.

But only what is essential.

Then:

Under-paint with the dominant colour.

Thin before thick paint.

Cool colour before warm.

Now:

Gradually modify tones and colours.

Use tone to show depth (perspective) – lightest and darkest tone closest with grey most distant.

Continue:

Refocus on the dominant colour and modify local colour accordingly.

Scumble the complementary (opposite) colours in light brushstrokes one on top of the other.

Use soft and hard edges for modelling.

Suggest texture by dry-brush or sgraffito techniques and under-paint beforehand.

Develop your experiment but do NOT overwork it.

Conclude:

Clean up.

UNIT 3: Experiment 3

Imagine two semi-abstracted MMM images to start.

Consider the visual element: Direction

The factor that indicates aim or course of movement.

Direction relates to a plane or axis, which may be horizontal, vertical or oblique.

There is a start and an end and can be seen in a serial order or sequence.

Materials:

Choice non-paint, opaque or transparent paint (dark, light, dominant, complementary) colours.

Three brushes (if using paint), white toned or coloured paper (a little larger).

Preparation:

Distort the portraits from the MMM images in your experiment.

Add two or more overlapping and distorted images (not portrait) into the experiment.

Decide the dominant colour.

Consider the tonal arrangement.

Think about the spaces

Begin:

Concentrate on the basic construction of your experiment.

Paint unimportant areas before important parts.

But only what is essential.

Then:

Under-paint with the dominant colour.

Thin before thick paint.

Cool colour before warm.

Now:

Gradually modify tones and colours.

Use tone to show depth (perspective) – lightest and darkest tone closest with grey most distant.

Continue:

Refocus on the dominant colour and modify local colour accordingly.

Use a pointillist technique - complementary (opposite) colours in small dots next to each other.

Use soft and hard edges for modelling.

Suggest texture by dry-brush or sgraffito techniques and under-paint beforehand.

Develop your experiment but do NOT overwork it.

Conclude:

Clean up.

UNIT 3: Experiment 4

Imagine two semi-abstracted MMM images to start.

Consider the visual element: Direction

The factor that indicates aim or course of movement.

Direction relates to a plane or axis, which may be horizontal, vertical or oblique.

Materials:

Choice dark, light, dominant, complementary colours (two harmonious one complementary).

Three brushes (if using paint), white toned or coloured paper (a little larger).

Preparation:

Distort the portraits from the MMM images in your experiment.

Add two or more overlapping and distorted images (not portrait) into the experiment.

Imagine some reflections of the semi-abstract portrait images.

Decide the colour scheme (two harmonious one complementary).

Consider the tonal arrangement.

Think about the spaces

Begin:

Concentrate on the basic construction of your experiment.

Paint unimportant areas before important parts.

But only what is essential.

Then:

Under-paint with the dominant colour.

Thin before thick paint.

Cool colour before warm.

Now:

Gradually modify tones and colours.

Use tone to show depth (perspective) – lightest and darkest tone closest with grey most distant.

Reflections are upside down images.

If the surface is disturbed (water) reflections are darker.

A shiny or glossy surface takes some of the reflected local colour.

Continue:

Refocus on the dominant colour and modify local colour accordingly.

Use a pointillist technique - complementary (opposite) colours in small dots next to each other.

Use soft and hard edges for modelling.

Suggest texture by dry-brush or sgraffito techniques and under-paint beforehand.

Develop your experiment but do NOT overwork it.

Conclude:

Clean up.

UNIT 3: Experiment 5

Imagine two semi-abstracted MMM images to start.

Consider the visual element: Direction

The factor that indicates aim or course of movement.

Materials:

Choice dark, light, dominant, complementary colours (two harmonious one complementary).

The colours should be different from those used in the last experiment.

Three brushes (if using paint), white toned or coloured paper (a little larger).

Preparation:

Distort the portraits from the MMM images in your experiment.

Add two or more overlapping and distorted images (not portrait) into the experiment.

Imagine some reflections of the semi-abstract portrait images.

Decide the colour scheme (two harmonious one complementary) but different from previously.

Consider the tonal arrangement.

Think about the spaces

Begin:

Concentrate on the basic construction of your experiment.

Paint unimportant areas before important parts.

But only what is essential.

Then:

Under-paint with the dominant colour.

Thin before thick paint.

Cool colour before warm.

Now:

Gradually modify tones and colours.

Use tone to show depth (perspective) – lightest and darkest tone closest with grey most distant.

Reflections are upside down images.

If the surface is disturbed (water) reflections are darker.

A shiny or glossy surface takes some of the reflected local colour.

Continue:

Refocus on the dominant colour and modify local colour accordingly.

Use a pointillist technique - complementary (opposite) colours in small dots next to each other.

Use soft and hard edges for modelling.

Suggest texture by dry-brush or sgraffito techniques and under-paint beforehand.

Develop your experiment but do NOT overwork it.

Conclude:

Clean up.

UNIT 3: Experiment 6

Imagine two semi-abstracted MMM images to start.

Consider the visual element: Direction

The factor that indicates aim or course of movement.

Materials:

Choice dark, light, dominant, complementary colours (two harmonious one complementary).

The colours should be different from those used in the last experiment.

Three brushes (if using paint), white toned or coloured paper (a little larger).

Preparation:

Distort the portraits from the MMM images in your experiment.

Add two or more overlapping and distorted images (not portrait) into the experiment.

Imagine some reflections of the semi-abstract portrait images.

Decide the colour scheme (two harmonious one complementary) but different from previously.

Consider the tonal arrangement.

Think about the spaces

Begin:

Concentrate on the basic construction of your experiment.

Paint unimportant areas before important parts.

But only what is essential.

Then:

Under-paint with the dominant colour.

Thin before thick paint.

Cool colour before warm.

Now:
Gradually modify tones and colours.
Use tone to show depth (perspective) – lightest and darkest tone closest with grey most distant.
Reflections are upside down images.
If the surface is disturbed (water) reflections are darker.
A shiny or glossy surface takes some of the reflected local colour.

Continue:
Refocus on the dominant colour and modify local colour accordingly.
Use a pointillist technique - complementary (opposite) colours in small dots next to each other.
Use soft and hard edges for modelling.
Suggest texture by dry-brush or sgraffito techniques and under-paint beforehand.
Develop your experiment but do NOT overwork it.
Conclude:
Clean up.

Further thoughts:
Also continue to experiment so that the portrait is totally abstract.
In other words it is just a shape within the experiment.
Continue to vary the viewpoint of your imaginary portrait.

DEVELOPMENT: Extensions

In the Development extension activities:

Draw on what you have learnt.

You can link what you have learned to your own goals.

DEVELOPMENT: Extension 1

Imagine a distorted MMM image to start.

Materials:

Use the SAME materials as used in a previous experiment from Unit One.

Use the SAME MMM image as used in a previous experiment Unit One.

Begin:

BUT repeat only one of the experiments.

DEVELOPMENT: Extension 2

Imagine a semi-abstract MMM image to start.

Materials:

Use the SAME materials as used in a previous experiment from Unit Two.

Use the SAME MMM image as used in a previous experiment Unit Two.

Begin:

BUT repeat only one of the experiments.

DEVELOPMENT: Extension 3

Imagine an abstract MMM image to start.

Materials:
Use the SAME materials as used in a previous experiment from Unit Three.
Use the SAME MMM image as used in a previous experiment Unit Three.
Begin:
BUT repeat only one of the experiments.

CONGRATULATIONS.

You have taken the IMAGINATION pathway.
This continues from the previous pattern of experiments.
Your imagination is a basis for a continuing search for a personal reality.
This is the final step to being the artist you want to be.

Your MMM experiments are like the athletes training program.
Like an Olympic athlete you want to be at the highest level so keep training.
Your MMM experiments become a normal routine.

Make notes, do sketches and record what you can see.
This is material you can draw on when continuing your MMM experiments.
Make a habit to carry a small sketchpad or scraps of paper and a pen or pencil.

Start each day with a short period of experiments.
Then move to your main artistic tasks.

You'll need to construct YOUR OWN MMM experimental programs.
By now this should not be difficult.

Planning major works could follow from that.
But do them as extensions of your MMM experiments.
A slightly larger experiment can develop into a major work.
Then much of the planning and preparatory work has been done.

WHERE NEXT?

You can buy an e-book:
Which is always the latest version.
OR
A printed book which is current at the time of purchase.
But will NOT be updated in the future.

There are other books that link with this book.
BUT they have a different focus.
You can specialize by completing ONE of the books.
But you can also complete as many of these books as you wish.
That could even be at different times.

Animals
http://www.amazon.com/dp/B08CP92NMW

Buildings
http://www.amazon.com/dp/B08CPJJTJS

Figures
http://www.amazon.com/dp/B08CPDL76B

Flowers
http://www.amazon.com/dp/B08CPLDRVT

Landscapes
http://www.amazon.com/dp/B08CPBJY1G

Still Life
http://www.amazon.com/dp/B08CPLLXRB

An Art Program is a background this book.
http://www.amazon.com/dp/1731347324
An Art Program book.
http://www.amazon.com/dp/B09GQSNY86

NOT NOW:

Perhaps one of these books could interest you then?

Publish your own memories?
http://www.amazon.com/dp/B087DWKPTP

A simple way to start developing creativity.
If you are a parent, teacher or who meet a group regularly?
http://www.amazon.com/dp/B088T1KFQZ

Start an art career.
But it's NOW is harder than it ever was.
To help someone start – they download this link.
http://www.amazon.com/dp/B088T7VJ76

More of my memories
http://www.amazon.com/dp/B087DWKPTP

SEND TO:

Know anyone interested in chocolate recipes?
Send them a link then.
http://www.amazon.com/dp/B088Y4RPL9

What about THIS book – portraits?
http://www.amazon.com/dp/B08CPLDRW3